MACAT

C000084239

An Analysis of

Frantz Fanon's

The Wretched
of the Earth

Riley Quinn

ROUTLEDGE

www.macat.com
info@macat.com

Cover illustration: Capucine Deslouis

Cataloguing in Publication Data
A catalogue record for this book is available from the British Library.
Library of Congress Cataloguing-in-Publication Data is available upon request.

ISBN 978-1-912303-74-8 (hardback)
ISBN 978-1-912128-53-2 (paperback)
ISBN 978-1-912282-62-3 (e-book)

Notice
The information in this book is designed to orientate readers of the work under analysis,
to elucidate and contextualise its key ideas and themes, and to aid in the development
of critical thinking skills. It is not meant to be used, nor should it be used, as a
substitute for original thinking or in place of original writing or research. References and
notes are provided for informational purposes and their presence does not constitute
endorsement of the information or opinions therein. This book is presented solely for
educational purposes. It is sold on the understanding that the publisher is not engaged
to provide any scholarly advice. The publisher has made every effort to ensure that
this book is accurate and up-to-date, but makes no warranties or representations with
regard to the completeness or reliability of the information it contains. The information
and the opinions provided herein are not guaranteed or warranted to produce particular
results and may not be suitable for students of every ability. The publisher shall not be
liable for any loss, damage or disruption arising from any errors or omissions, or from
the use of this book, including, but not limited to, special, incidental, consequential or
other damages caused, or alleged to have been caused, directly or indirectly, by the
information contained within.

CONTENTS

THE MACAT LIBRARY

The Macat Library is a series of unique academic explorations of seminal works in the humanities and social sciences – books and papers that have had a significant and widely recognised impact on their disciplines. It has been created to serve as much more than just a summary of what lies between the covers of a great book. It illuminates and explores the influences on, ideas of, and impact of that book. Our goal is to offer a learning resource that encourages critical thinking and fosters a better, deeper understanding of important ideas.

Each publication is divided into three Sections: Influences, Ideas, and Impact. Each Section has four Modules. These explore every important facet of the work, and the responses to it.

This Section-Module structure makes a Macat Library book easy to use, but it has another important feature. Because each Macat book is written to the same format, it is possible (and encouraged!) to cross-reference multiple Macat books along the same lines of inquiry or research. This allows the reader to open up interesting interdisciplinary pathways.

To further aid your reading, lists of glossary terms and people mentioned are included at the end of this book (these are indicated by an asterisk [*] throughout) – as well as a list of works cited.

Macat has worked with the University of Cambridge to identify the elements of critical thinking and understand the ways in which six different skills combine to enable effective thinking.
Three allow us to fully understand a problem; three more give us the tools to solve it. Together, these six skills make up the **PACIER** model of critical thinking. They are:

ANALYSIS – understanding how an argument is built
EVALUATION – exploring the strengths and weaknesses of an argument
INTERPRETATION – understanding issues of meaning

CREATIVE THINKING – coming up with new ideas and fresh connections
PROBLEM-SOLVING – producing strong solutions
REASONING – creating strong arguments

To find out more, visit **WWW.MACAT.COM.**

CRITICAL THINKING AND *THE WRETCHED OF THE EARTH*

Primary critical thinking skill: REASONING
Secondary critical thinking skill: CREATIVE THINKING

Frantz Fanon is one of the most important figures in the history of what is now known as postcolonial studies – the field that examines the meaning and impacts of European colonialism across the world.

Born in the French colony of Martinique, Fanon worked as a psychiatrist in Algeria, another French colony that saw brutal violence during its revolution against French rule. His experiences power the searing indictment of colonialism that is his final book, 1961's *The Wretched of the Earth*. Fanon's account of the physical and psychological violence of colonialism forms the basis of a passionate, closely reasoned call to arms – a call for violent revolution. Incendiary even today, it was more so in its time; the book first during the brutal conflict caused by the Algerian Revolution. Viewed as a profoundly dangerous work by the colonial powers of the world, Fanon's book helped to inspire liberation struggles across the globe.

Though it has flaws, *The Wretched of the Earth* is above all a testament to the power of passionately sustained and closely reasoned argument: Fanon's presentation of his evidence combines with his passion to produce an argument that it is almost impossible not to be swayed by.

ABOUT THE AUTHOR OF THE ORIGINAL WORK

The psychiatrist **Frantz Fanon** was born in 1925 and grew up in Martinique, which was a French colony at the time. His first book, 1952's *Black Skin, White Masks*, was a condemnation of colonial racism that explored the causes and effects of racial prejudice.

As Fanon got older he became increasingly radical, partly because of his involvement in the Algerian War of Independence against France. But he died young, in 1961 aged just 36, from leukemia. It was mainly after his death that his academic contribution was recognized and appreciated.

ABOUT THE AUTHOR OF THE ANALYSIS

Riley Quinn holds master's degrees in politics and international relations from both LSE and the University of Oxford.

ABOUT MACAT

GREAT WORKS FOR CRITICAL THINKING

Macat is focused on making the ideas of the world's great thinkers accessible and comprehensible to everybody, everywhere, in ways that promote the development of enhanced critical thinking skills.

It works with leading academics from the world's top universities to produce new analyses that focus on the ideas and the impact of the most influential works ever written across a wide variety of academic disciplines. Each of the works that sit at the heart of its growing library is an enduring example of great thinking. But by setting them in context – and looking at the influences that shaped their authors, as well as the responses they provoked – Macat encourages readers to look at these classics and game-changers with fresh eyes. Readers learn to think, engage and challenge their ideas, rather than simply accepting them.

'Macat offers an amazing first-of-its-kind tool for interdisciplinary learning and research. Its focus on works that transformed their disciplines and its rigorous approach, drawing on the world's leading experts and educational institutions, opens up a world-class education to anyone.'

Andreas Schleicher
Director for Education and Skills, Organisation for Economic
Co-operation and Development

'Macat is taking on some of the major challenges in university education … They have drawn together a strong team of active academics who are producing teaching materials that are novel in the breadth of their approach.'

Prof Lord Broers,
former Vice-Chancellor of the University of Cambridge

'The Macat vision is exceptionally exciting. It focuses upon new modes of learning which analyse and explain seminal texts which have profoundly influenced world thinking and so social and economic development. It promotes the kind of critical thinking which is essential for any society and economy.
This is the learning of the future.'

Rt Hon Charles Clarke, former UK Secretary of State for Education

'The Macat analyses provide immediate access to the critical conversation surrounding the books that have shaped their respective discipline, which will make them an invaluable resource to all of those, students and teachers, working in the field.'

Professor William Tronzo, University of California at San Diego

WAYS IN TO THE TEXT

KEY POINTS

- Frantz Fanon was an influential theorist and writer born in the French colony of Martinique in 1925.

- His personal experiences of racism and colonialism* (the political domination and exploitation of one nation by another) directly affected his work as a writer and thinker.

- His 1961 book *The Wretched of the Earth* analyses the effects of colonialism on the colonized and sets down a powerful argument for the violent overthrow of colonial regimes by their victims.

Who Was Frantz Fanon?

Frantz Fanon, the author of *The Wretched of the Earth* (1961), was born in 1925 in Martinique, an island in the Caribbean and, from 1635, a colony of France. Fanon's family was middle class. His father was a civil servant and his mother owned a shop. His belief in liberty drove him to enlist in the Free French army, a force composed of volunteers and troops outside the borders of occupied France, formed to fight Nazi* Germany and its allies in World War II* (1939–45). Fanon's experiences in the French military exposed him to real racism. He no longer thought of himself as Martiniquais (a Martinique national), but as a black man, who faced abuse himself and saw it perpetrated on others. Fanon went home to Martinique after the war, but soon returned to France to study medicine at Lyon University, where he specialized in psychiatry.

Fanon began his career in France, but in 1953 he moved to the North African nation of Algeria, becoming chief of staff at a mental hospital in the city of Blida. Algeria was a French colony at the time and the Algerians suffered many abuses at the hands of the French until, in 1954, they rebelled. Fanon supported the revolution, but continued to work at Blida until 1957, when he left for neighboring Tunisia. He continued to work in medicine, but also represented the new Algerian government abroad and became friends with the French philosopher Jean-Paul Sartre* during this period.

Fanon's death from cancer in 1961 came just months after completing this, his final book.

What Does *The Wretched of the Earth* Say?

The starting point of *The Wretched of the Earth* is violence. Fanon argues that, because colonialism is both created and sustained by violence, it can be destroyed only by violence. For Fanon, violence serves a double purpose. First, it destroys the colonial system in the only possible way when just one side holds all the power and the weapons. Second, violence serves an important psychological purpose. Fanon believes that colonialism dehumanizes the colonized, who can reassert their true humanity only by violent action against the powers that dehumanize them. While Fanon's inquiry references the thought and analysis of the German political philosopher Karl Marx,* notably in his belief that history is a process of increasing freedom that progresses through conflict between the classes, he rejects Marxist* premises such as the idea that economic change alone produces change in society.

Fanon believed that the force behind any revolution is the "lumpenproletariat"* —rural peasants, the very worst off. Those who are middle class fail to rise up because they accept the colonizers' views and, more pragmatically, they have done too well under the colonial regime; if they were to lead the revolution, the new government would be similar to the old one, and even if they were to rise up, they would retain close links with their colonizers. This scenario would mean decolonization and a change in government, but no real social change. Fanon says decolonization is not about negotiation, because that would lack the necessary cathartic* violence.

He also holds strong views on how a postcolonial* country should be run. He is wary of nationalism* (the view that defining oneself as part of a certain nation is foremost, perhaps for the superiority that comes from belonging to that nation) and, indeed, the abstract idea of *the nation* itself. It may be useful for rallying support, he says, but nationalism is just another ideology that fails to bring about real change. The change Fanon wants is one of *real improvement* in the lives of the *worst off*. A government that focuses on nationalism rather than national consciousness (education, investment, improvement) is not revolutionary.

Fanon himself was both a psychiatrist and a revolutionary—as is evident in the final chapters of the book, in which he looks at the effects of colonialism on both the colonizers and the colonized. Colonialism itself, he says, is a source of mental illness. He cites two particularly powerful cases. One concerns two Algerian boys who killed a French playmate because their lives were filled with such abject hopelessness, and the other is the story of a French officer who became paranoid after engaging in torture. Fanon could not treat him, as it would just have enabled him to torture again.

Why Does *The Wretched of the Earth* Matter?

The Wretched of the Earth was written, in part, to inspire revolution. Fanon attacks the central assumption of colonialism: that colonized peoples are inferior to their colonizers. This idea might be based in direct racism—for instance, thinking that white Europeans are superior to the native populations of other continents. Or, less directly, it might be based on a belief that the colonized countries are less "evolved" or "civilized" than the colonizing powers. *Wretched* makes a strong argument against both views. It denies the power of colonial "experts" to claim with any authority that colonized people are inferior, and want or need colonialism.

Wretched influenced revolutionary movements around the world, and liberation struggles in South Africa, South America, and Iran, among many others. The book matters, and will continue to matter, because while direct colonialism may have ended, it can be argued that colonial abuse lives on. The West continues to dominate, both economically and militarily. Former colonies gain independence only to have the World Bank,* a financial institution that makes loans to developing nations, rewrite their economic policies to favor global companies. It is arguable whether many of the regimes that have replaced colonial governments (especially throughout the Middle East and Africa) have improved the lives of the worst off. Fanon's "lumpenproletariat" may have been betrayed by their fellow citizens.

The text has become an inspiration for postcolonialism studies. Postcolonial theory critiques colonial inequality and the representation of colonized people as inferior. The idea that non-Western, non-white people are inferior is, in fact, still pervasive, and postcolonialism seeks to undermine this notion. It also points to a new imperial project based on the United States' "War on Terror"* overseas and the portrayal of Muslims as inherently dangerous that it endorses. Hamid Dabashi,* an Iranian American professor of literature, says that the desire to save Muslim societies from their own alleged barbarism is not so very dissimilar to the idea that, for example, Algerians are inferior and cannot govern themselves. *The Wretched of the Earth* reminds us not only how wrong these ideas are, but how damaging they can be.

SECTION 1
INFLUENCES

MODULE 1
THE AUTHOR AND THE
HISTORICAL CONTEXT

KEY POINTS

- Frantz Fanon's *The Wretched of the Earth* argues that only violence can destroy colonial* rule, both politically and in the psyche—the mind—of the colonized.

- Fanon was born on the Caribbean island of Martinique and, after studying medicine in France, became a psychiatrist in the North African nation of Algeria, where he supported the revolution against colonial domination by France.

- For centuries, colonialism and racism were widespread around the globe. While the second half of the twentieth century saw widespread decolonization, both colonialism and racism remain a fact of life for many.

Why Read This Text?

The Wretched of the Earth by Frantz Fanon (1961) is a manifesto for the Third World* (as developing nations were then known). It was one of the original works of anticolonial theory as well as the postcolonial* theory that followed—a theory that seeks to critique the various cultural, social, and political legacies of colonialism. Repudiating the idea that Europeans have a right to dominate non-Europeans because of the mistaken belief that they are somehow inferior, the book is as much an inspiration for the cause of freedom today as it was when it was written.

Although Fanon wrote the text during the Algerian War of Independence,* during which the nation fought for political autonomy from colonial France, its basis was a lifetime's experience of

14

> **❝ Who was this recently married young man who turned up in Algeria under clearly circumscribed conventions to join the medical staff of a psychiatric hospital located in a subdivision of the capital city? ❞**
>
> Alice Cherki, *Frantz Fanon: A Portrait*

racial stereotyping by French colonial society. Fanon, a psychiatrist by profession, laid bare the inferiority complex that colonialism projected onto its lower orders. His answer to this, politically and psychologically, was violence. When violently occupied by a dehumanizing colonial force, Fanon insisted you had to respond in kind.

Essentially, then, *Wretched* is a call to arms. Fanon argued that the aim was liberation and that it could not be achieved by the colonized middle classes, as they would simply make a pact with the colonizer and society would continue unchanged. Instead, it was the peasants, the "wretched," who must find their own human dignity by destroying colonialism, root and branch. The book has gone on to influence numerous struggles by the dispossessed, especially those fighting racism.[1]

Author's Life

Fanon was born in 1925 on Martinique, a Caribbean island colonized by the French in 1635 and still officially part of France today—it is designated an "overseas region" (*Région d'outre-mer*) with all the powers of the regions of mainland France and the euro as its currency. He was born into a middle-class family—his father was a civil servant and his mother owned a hardware store.[2] Fanon enlisted in the Free French army in 1943, an army opposing both the occupying German forces in France and the French Vichy* government, which was little more than a puppet of the Nazis.*

15

During World War II, Fanon was stationed in Algiers, the capital of Algeria—another French colony—in North Africa. It was here that he was first exposed to racist abuse, and witnessed a local population reduced to "picking through the leftovers" in the rubbish outside the barracks for food.[3] On returning to Martinique, he worked for the election campaign of the poet and social reformer Aimé Césaire,* the Communist candidate for mayor in the island's capital, Fort-de-France. Césaire had been Fanon's secondary school teacher and had a profound influence on him.

Fanon's stay in Martinique did not last long. In 1945, he traveled to Lyon, in mainland France, to study medicine. Specializing in psychiatry, he graduated in 1950.[4] In 1953, he returned to Algeria, working at the Blida-Joinville Psychiatric Hospital. When the Algerian War of Independence broke out in 1954, Fanon found himself treating both members of the nationalist pro-independence party, *Front de Libération Nationale* (FLN),* and French officers psychologically damaged by killing and torturing them.[5] He was expelled from Algeria due to his support for the FLN and went to Tunisia, where he continued to support and work for the organization.[6]

In 1961, Fanon was diagnosed with leukemia, prompting him to write with renewed urgency, knowing he did not have long to live. That same year, in Italy, he met the influential French philosophers Jean-Paul Sartre* and Simone de Beauvoir,* the latter noted for her contribution to feminist* thought. Sartre was already an influence; the French philosopher had published much of Fanon's work in his journal *Les Temps modernes* ("Modern Times").[7] Fanon asked Sartre to write the preface to *The Wretched of the Earth*.

Fanon died in December 1961, shortly before Algeria was liberated. *Wretched* was published just a few days before his death.

Author's Background

The Wretched of the Earth was written in 1961 in the midst of a global "decolonization"* movement. The European powers had maintained empires across the world, in South America, the Caribbean, North America, Africa, and Asia, but they had been considerably weakened by World War II* both economically and politically, and began to shed their global colonies.[8]

Decolonization, however, was not a smooth process. Algeria, for example, where Fanon would spend his later years, was officially part of "Metropolitan France"—that is, a region with the same powers as anywhere on the mainland. Its population at the time of eight million people included a million Europeans,[9] but the native Algerians had fought long and hard against inequality, arbitrary arrest, and their status as second-class citizens. The historian Gary Wilder* notes that the stereotype of Africans—either "big children" or "dangerous savages"— meant the French believed they were "too immature to exercise political rights responsibly."[10] So the debate during decolonization was about the ability of colonies to govern themselves—a discussion that slowed down movements to independence.

Algeria used violence to secure its independence. The FLN rose up against the French in 1954, striking targets in Algeria and in France. The French response included torture and murder, often against civilians.[11] Fanon's open support for the FLN began in 1956, when he resigned his post at the hospital in Blida where he worked. In his resignation letter, Fanon wrote, "I owe it to myself to affirm that the Arab, permanently an alien in his own country, lives in a state of absolute depersonalization"[12] (a term implying that Arab citizens were denied their individuality and, by extension, their status as human beings). By the time the conflict ended with the Evian Agreement* in 1962 between France and the Provisional Government of the Algerian Republic, the death toll was estimated at 1.5 million.

NOTES

1   Edmund Burke III, "Frantz Fanon's 'The Wretched of the Earth'," *Daedalus* 105, no. 1 (1976): 127.

2   David Macey, *Frantz Fanon: A Biography* (London: Verso, 2012), 55.

3   Alice Cherki, *Frantz Fanon: A Portrait*, trans. Nadia Benabid (Ithaca, NY: Cornell University Press, 2006), 11.

4   Cherki, *Frantz Fanon*, 16–17.

5   Cherki, *Frantz Fanon*, 78–9.

6   Macey, *Frantz Fanon*, 296.

7   Macey, *Frantz Fanon*, 454.

8   Muriel Chamberlain, *Longman Companion to European Decolonisation in the Twentieth* Century (Oxford: Routledge, 2013), 7.

9   Chamberlain, *Longman Companion*, 8.

10 Gary Wilder, *The French Imperial Nation State: Negritude and Colonial Humanism Between the Two World Wars* (Chicago: University of Chicago Press, 2005), 126.

11 Macey, *Frantz Fanon*, 246.

12 Frantz Fanon, "Letter to the Resident Minister," in *Toward The African Revolution*, trans. Haakon Chevalier (New York: Grove Press, 1965), 53.

MODULE 2
ACADEMIC CONTEXT

KEY POINTS

- The core ethical question of colonialism,* the political dominance of one nation by another, is "Can the exploitation of others ever be justified?"

- The colonial debate has addressed questions of its moral permissibility, its roots in economic exploitation, and its psychological effects.

- Fanon was profoundly influenced by the *négritude** movement, a social and literary current created by artists who sought to reclaim "blackness" as "goodness."

The Work in its Context

Frantz Fanon's *The Wretched of the Earth* takes a position in a discussion about colonialism as old as colonialism itself. In 1550, a debate took place in Valladolid,* in Spain, between Bishop Bartolomé de las Casas* and the Spanish philosopher Juan Ginés de Sepúlveda* concerning whether or not Spain should continue to conquer the New World and subjugate its natives. Las Casas argued that the Spanish should respect the natives' humanity, as they "were reasonable men governing themselves in reasonable ways," and their potential to become Christians made them the spiritual equals of Europeans.[1] Sepúlveda used the ancient Greek philosopher Aristotle* to justify the opposite position. Aristotle, in his *Politics*, suggested that slavery can be natural. He argued that some people, inferior in mental capacity and reason, are fit only to work and it was for their own benefit that they should be slaves to better men. Sepúlveda argued that, as the natives were neither Christian nor civilized, they were natural slaves and should be regarded as the property of Spain.[2]

66 Between colonizer and colonized there is room only for forced labor, intimidation, pressure, the police, taxation, theft, rape, compulsory crops, contempt, mistrust, arrogance, self-complacency, swinishness, brainless elites, degraded masses. 99

Aimé Césaire, *Discourse on Colonialism*

While this debate occurred in the sixteenth century, the same fundamental concerns would continue into postcolonial* literature and theory: "The assumption of postcolonial studies," writes the social theorist Robert C. Young,* "is that many of the wrongs, if not crimes, against humanity are a product of the economic dominance of the north [Europe and later North America] over the South [Africa, Asia, and South America]."[3] Postcolonial writing aims to reveal the "forces of oppression and coercive domination" that operate in the contemporary world, whether actual political regimes (such as the French in Algeria, who were of particular concern to Fanon) or the portrayal of non-Western/nonwhite people as inferior (as Sepúlveda would have argued).[4]

Overview of the Field

After the Italian explorer Christopher Columbus* set sail in 1492, Europe began to take control of more and more of the world and the unequal relationship at the heart of colonialism became the subject of fierce debate. In the eighteenth century, the British philosopher Jeremy Bentham* addressed his pamphlet *Emancipate Your Colonies* to the French: "You choose your own government, why are not other people to choose theirs? ... What is become of the rights of men? Are you the only men who have rights?"[5] The premise of this critique was that Europeans and non-Europeans are equal and so have equal rights. The main counterargument to this point, represented by John Stuart

Mill,* was that Europe had a responsibility to "civilize" people who were "savage."[6]

In the following century, the German political philosopher Karl Marx's* *Das Kapital* attacked the exploitation inherent in the economic and social system of capitalism,* in which trade and industry are held in private hands and conducted for private profit. Marx based his theory on the idea that freedom grows slowly over the course of history due to conflict between the social classes. There is always a dominant class, which controls the means of production (the resources and tools required for labor). Under the system of feudalism,* the aristocracy controlled the land. Under capitalism, the bourgeoisie*—the middle classes with money to invest—owned the factories. Marx saw both of these assets as the economic "base" or means of production in their societies. For Marx, this base was the source of religion, ideology, and culture—the "superstructure." The superstructure merely existed, however, to justify the exploitation of the lower class (the proletariat). Only revolution would move society forward.

The Russian revolutionary Vladimir Lenin* took Marx's theory and applied it to imperialism* (the ideology and practice of empire building). In his *Imperialism Is the Highest Stage of Capitalism*, he argued that capitalism would eventually need to find new territories for its capital and new markets that could sustain growth. Imperialists were, therefore, "parasites" on their colonies[7] and colonialism becomes a necessary stage in the growth of capitalism.

By the twentieth century, an analysis emerged of what it means—psychologically and socially—to be the colonized in a world dominated by colonizers. The US social theorist W. E. B. Du Bois* wrote that to be black in the United States was to experience a life of "double consciousness." This meant "looking at one's self through the eyes of others ... measuring one's soul by the tape of a world that looks on in amused contempt and pity."[8] In other words, while black people see themselves *as themselves*, they also measure their worth by a white yardstick of what is "normal," or "desirable." This is the psychological result of absolute domination: they are torn between being themselves and intrinsically worthwhile, and trying to imitate their dominators.

Academic Influences

Of Fanon's many influences, two are particularly important: the Martiniquan poet and political figure Aimé Césaire* and the French intellectual Jean-Paul Sartre.* Césaire's *Discourse on Colonialism* attacked colonialism for "decivilizing" the colonized to justify abuse and exploitation.[9] He wrote that so-called "savage" societies outside Europe had complex cultures, well-developed (and functional) political institutions, and other worthwhile features.[10] European colonial discourse*—that is, the language used to discuss, and influenced by, the colonial relationship—entails convincing colonized people that their civilization is inferior because it is non-European, which, for Césaire, is an absurdity. Césaire's philosophy—that of the social and literary movement called *négritude*—held that "blackness" was inherently valuable, and that being African was a source of great cultural worth.

Jean-Paul Sartre also wrote on *négritude*. On the movement's poetry he said, "These black men are addressing themselves to black men about black men," meaning the poetry did not seek the approval, or even the reaction, of white readers. Such poetry, he continued, "is neither satiric nor imprecatory: it is an awakening to consciousness."[11] What does Sartre mean by this? He is saying that black artists are forging a distinctive identity, and awakening to their own humanity, which had for so long been questioned by whites. *Négritude* was an artistic philosophy, but it reclaimed ownership of black lives and identities.

NOTES

1 Sacvan Bercovitch, ed., *The Cambridge History of American Literature: Volume I 1590–1820* (Cambridge: Cambridge University Press, 1994), 48.

2 Bercovitch, *Cambridge History*, 48.

3 Robert J. C. Young, *Postcolonialism: An Historical Introduction* (Oxford: Blackwell, 2001), 6.

4 Young, *Postcolonialism*, 11.

5 Jeremy Bentham, *Emancipate Your Colonies: Addressed to the National Convention of France* (London: Robert Heward, 1830), 3.

6 Eileen Sullivan, "Liberalism and Imperialism: J. S. Mill's Defence of the British Empire," *Journal of the History of Ideas* 44, no. 4 (1983): 607–9.

7 Vladimir Lenin, *Imperialism: The Highest Stage of Capitalism* (Sydney: Resistance Books, 1999), 100.

8 W. E. B Du Bois, *The Souls of Black Folk: The Oxford W. E. B. Du Bois, Volume 3*, ed. Henry Louis Gates, Jr. (Oxford: Oxford University Press, 2007), 3.

9 Robin D. G. Kelley, "Introduction," in *Discourse on Colonialism* by Aimé Césaire, trans. Joan Pinkham (New York: Monthly Review Press, 2000), 8–9.

10 Césaire, *Discourse on Colonialism*, 52.

11 Jean-Paul Sartre, "Black Orpheus," *Massachusetts Review* 6, no. 1 (1964–5): 16.

MODULE 3
THE PROBLEM

KEY POINTS

- By the middle of the twentieth century, many people were questioning the propriety of colonialism.* While the United Nations* demanded self-government for the colonies, those following race-based theories of intelligence still argued that colonized people were unable to govern themselves.

- The French psychologist Octave Mannoni* and the Tunisian author and cultural theorist Albert Memmi* both produced analyses of colonial psychology and the relationship between colonizer and colonized.

- Fanon rejected the arguments of race scientists and Mannoni alike; for him, they all placed too much responsibility for colonial problems on the colonized.

Core Question

Frantz Fanon's *The Wretched of the Earth* was published at a time when European colonialism was under growing scrutiny and being increasingly questioned; the 1945 charter of the United Nations had helped set the stage for the postcolonial* era, establishing "the principle that the interests of the inhabitants of these [colonial] territories are paramount," and that in accordance with "the political aspirations of the peoples" they will "develop self-government."[1] The question was how to interpret this principle. Fanon's core mission in *Wretched* was not so much to answer the question as to advance an agenda—"a complete calling into question of the colonial situation."[2] We might compare this to the Russian revolutionary Vladimir Lenin's* *What is to be Done?*, the 1901 pamphlet that called for a vanguard of

❝ The Algerian has no cortex. ❞

Antoine Porot, quoted in *The Wretched of the Earth*

intellectuals to persuade Russian workers to adopt the political philosophy of Marxism* and revolution.

Fanon questioned colonialism on the basis that all human beings are fundamentally equal. This idea was not entirely accepted, as theories of racial hierarchy were common—including in the medical profession. For example, Antoine Porot* of the Algiers School of Neuropsychiatry* held that "there is no inner life where the North African is concerned," because they lacked higher brain function.[3] In other words, he suggested that faulty biology enabled one race to claim superiority to, and legitimize its dominance of, others. Fanon goes on to cite the British doctor J. C. Carothers,* who concluded that "the African," while physically the same, "makes very little use of his frontal lobes," suggesting he is akin to a "lobotomized European."[4] This view sought to turn colonial resistance into mental illness. Fanon and his fellow thinkers responded that, on the contrary, it would be madder to submit to colonial dominance than resist it.

The Participants

The French psychologist Octave Mannoni's *Prospero and Caliban* (1950) explored the psychological relationship between the French colonial administration on the island of Madagascar and the Malagasy natives. Mannoni, notably, was interested in the psychology of both the colonizer and the colonized, and the colonial situation that was the result of "misunderstanding, of mutual incomprehension" between them.[5] From the point of view of the colonizer, Mannoni argues, the relationship of white master and native subject exists before the two ever meet: the European psyche must project its own infantile and dangerous nature on others it encounters.[6]

On the colonized side, Mannoni argues that colonialism was "unconsciously expected—even desired—by the future subject peoples," who find liberation difficult and intimidating.[7] Mannoni is not justifying colonialism, but suggesting that the colonial relationship is "everyone's fault." In other words, Europeans take advantage of the dependency complex of the native population in order to dominate them. The European state of mind is "perfectly happy if we can project fantasies of our own unconscious on the outside world." If, though, Europeans then discover that the subjects of those fantasies "are not pure projections but real beings with claims of liberty," the domination of them appears outrageous.[8]

Mannoni advocates a gradual end to colonialism, but the cultural theorist Albert Memmi—author of *The Colonizer and the Colonized*— argues that "for the colonized, just as for the colonizer, there is no way out other than a complete end to colonization ... not only revolt, but a revolution."[9] Memmi, a Tunisian Jew, and therefore occupying a privileged position "between" the French occupiers and the Muslim natives, explored the relationship between the two. He argued that colonization justifies and maintains itself by highlighting the differences between the colonizer and the colonized, in such a way as to emphasize the superiority of the colonizer, and making those differences seem absolute, complete, and inevitable.[10] Colonial "good intentions," Memmi argues, are usually based on racist theory and little more than shallow justifications for denying the legitimate rights of the colonized.[11] The colonized, on the other hand, accept this situation, but only for a time. They initially believe the dehumanizing justification of colonialism, and will first attempt to imitate the colonizer. On the inevitable failure of this effort, however, they "will revolt."[12]

The Contemporary Debate

Fanon rejected the "scientific" racism of those who argued for the inferiority of certain peoples: "Today every one of us knows that criminality is not the consequence [of any innate characteristic of the Algerian]," he wrote.[13] He argued instead that Algerian violence was a product of dehumanization, of colonial society systematically pushing people to the edge. "In the [Algerian] concentration camps," Fanon wrote, "men killed each other for a bit of bread."[14] The colonial system left its victims equally desperate.

Fanon roundly criticizes Mannoni's theory of colonialism in his earlier *Black Skin, White Masks* (1952), where he argues that Mannoni "leaves the Malagasy no choice save between inferiority and dependence."[15] By positioning himself solely in the realm of psychology, Mannoni fails to grasp the economic or political circumstances. Fanon argues strongly that the colonized do not simply have the choice of whether to "turn white or disappear." Instead, they should be "put into a position to choose action ... with respect to the real source of the conflict—that is, toward the social structures."[16]

On the relationship between Fanon and Memmi, Fanon's principal biographer David Macey* writes that there is "no indication" that Fanon ever read Memmi's work. He suggests that "the similarity between their respective analyses of the colonial situation" is a result of their shared relationship with Jean-Paul Sartre.*[17]

NOTES

1   United Nations, *Charter of the United Nations*, Article 73, October 24, 1945, accessed October 2, 2015, www.un.org/en/documents/charter/chapter11.shtml.

2   Frantz Fanon, *The Wretched of the Earth*, trans. Constance Farrington (London: Penguin, 2001), 28.

3   Antoine Porot, paraphrased in Frantz Fanon, *Wretched*, 242.

4   J. C. Carothers, paraphrased in Frantz Fanon, *Wretched*, 243.

5   Octave Mannoni, *Prospero and Caliban: The Psychology of Colonization*, trans. Pamela Powesland (Ann Arbor: University of Michigan Press, 1990), 31.

6   Mannoni, *Prospero and Caliban*, 108.

7   Mannoni, *Prospero and Caliban*, 65, 86.

8   Mannoni, *Prospero and Caliban*, 117.

9   Albert Memmi, *The Colonizer and the Colonized* (Boston, MA: Beacon Press, 1991), 150.

10 Memmi, *Colonizer and Colonized*, 93.

11 Memmi, *Colonizer and Colonized*, 4.

12 Memmi, *Colonizer and Colonizer*, 120–7.

13 Fanon, *Wretched*, 247–8.

14 Fanon, *Wretched*, 248.

15 Frantz Fanon, *Black Skin, White Masks* (London: Pluto Press, 1986), 94.

16 Fanon, *Black Skin*, 100.

17 David Macey, *Frantz Fanon: A Biography* (London: Verso, 2012), 418.

MODULE 4
THE AUTHOR'S CONTRIBUTION

KEY POINTS

- *The Wretched of the Earth* is a political manifesto; its aim is to enable the colonized to reclaim their humanity through violence.

- Fanon takes a Marxist* approach, but extends it to encompass the colonial* situation as a special category.

- *Wretched* was heavily influenced by the work of Jean-Paul Sartre,* especially his *Critique of Dialectical Reason*.

Author's Aims

Frantz Fanon's *The Wretched of the Earth* is a political manifesto. "You do not turn any society … upside down," Fanon argues, "if you have not decided to from the very beginning."[1] Fanon wanted to spend the end of his life physically fighting with the Algerian independence movement *Front de Libération Nationale* (FLN),* but "the Algerian leadership … paid no heed to this request," so he transferred his fury to the page.[2] Fanon knew he was dying when he wrote *Wretched*, and intended to leave the strongest possible statement of his vision for the Third World.*[3]

Fanon's local aims for Algeria need to be understood in relation to this global project. The book looks beyond Algeria, discussing the whole "Third World" as a monolith, "facing Europe," whose underlying unity is based on the need for resistance against colonialism.[4] "What does Fanon care," Jean-Paul Sartre asks in the introduction, "whether you [Europeans] read his work or not? It is to his brothers that he denounces our old tricks."[5] Fanon, in other words, is both fighting a war of ideas and providing a roadmap for the rehumanization of the oppressed in the Third World.

> 66 If [Fanon] demonstrates the tactics of colonialism, the complex play of relations which unite and oppose the colonists to the people of the mother country, it is for his brothers; his aim is to teach them to beat us at our own game. 99
>
> Jean-Paul Sartre, "Preface," in *The Wretched of the Earth*

Approach

Fanon's approach is partially Marxist* in its understanding that the struggle between social classes both plays a central role in driving historical events and is central to the achievement of emancipation (freedom). Unlike Marx,* however, Fanon emphasizes the role of race; he also believes that "Marxist analysis should always be slightly stretched every time we have to do with the colonial problem."[6]

According to Marxist analysis, cultural institutions are explained by the underlying economic system; under feudalism,* for instance, the peasant must obey the knight, so "a reference to divine right* [the notion that authority is given by God] is necessary to legitimize this statutory difference."[7] In other words, cultural ideas about people flow from economic arrangements. In the colonial context, on the other hand, it is not only the economic arrangement that defines the settler as the ruler, but also racial identity: "you are rich because you are white, you are white because you are rich," and your status is determined by being "unlike the original inhabitants."[8] In other words, even if a colonial subject is successful, his or her rise through the economic categories is meaningless in terms of his or her position in colonial society because he or she remains nonwhite. In colonial society, the main category of analysis is race, not class. In traditional Marxism, the "superstructure" (those institutions in a culture produced by the economic system—divine right, for example) exists, as the medical sociologist Kate Reed* argued, to "manage consent." This means that the peasant believes in divine right just as much as the knight does.[9] Colonialist power structures, however, are not built on consent, but rule instead through "terror and despair."[10]

Contribution in Context

Fanon was profoundly influenced by the existential phenomenology* of the French philosopher Jean-Paul Sartre. This school of thought holds that our ideas about ourselves (for example, thinking of oneself as black) are the product of our lived experiences (being described as black by others). Fanon did not think of himself as black, but rather as Martiniquais (a Martinique national), and so he saw himself as distinct from Africans—until white French people referred to him merely as black. This explains his view that neither black people nor white people "are" a certain way, and it is their experiences of one another that produce these race-linked identities. If being tall or short meant one would experience life differently, then being tall or short would be connected to a height identity.

Wretched is seen as particularly closely linked to Jean-Paul Sartre's 1960 book *Critique of Dialectical Reason*,[11] his coming-to-terms with Marxism and his reservations about it. In particular, he rejects the idea that mankind is predetermined to develop in a particular direction through class struggle. For Marx, Sartre wrote, reason is "grounded on a fundamental claim" that destiny is defined by one thing and if that one thing (in Marx's case, class struggle) can be understood, then the nature of human destiny can be grasped. Marx and his followers "define a rationality of the world"[12] based on just one thing, but Sartre's criticism is that dialectical reason does not encompass the full scope and nature of human freedom. Sartre saw Marxism as a fundamental denial of every human being to define freedom—"human nature" being a choice to be made by every person.

One of the key concepts in Sartre's book is praxis,* meaning an idea that is put into action; according to Marxist philosophy, we can oppose

31

praxis to *theory*. The praxis Sartre was interested in was the "practical consciousness" of the casting off of chains and living with freedom as an objective.[13] The British philosopher Robert Bernasconi* says of the two writers, "Sartre would have found *The Wretched of the Earth* closer" to his own ideas "than anything he had written in the *Critique* precisely because Fanon's book emerged from action in process."[14] In other words, the call to revolution of Fanon's *Wretched* was an example of the "practical consciousness" advocated by Sartre. *Wretched* encouraged human freedom, not in the abstract but in the throwing off of chains.

NOTES

1   Frantz Fanon, *The Wretched of the Earth*, trans. Constance Farrington (London: Penguin, 2001), 28–9.

2   Alice Cherki, *Frantz Fanon: A Portrait*, trans. Nadia Benabid (Ithaca, NY: Cornell University Press, 2006), 157.

3   Cherki, *Frantz Fanon*, 159.

4   David Macey, *Frantz Fanon: A Biography* (London: Verso, 2012), 465.

5   Jean-Paul Sartre, "Introduction," in Fanon, *Wretched*, 11.

6   Fanon, *Wretched*, 31.

7   Fanon, *Wretched*, 31.

8   Fanon, *Wretched*, 31.

9   Kate Reed, *New Directions in Social Theory: Race, Gender, and the Canon* (London: Sage, 2006), 103.

10 Reed, *New Directions*, 104.

11 Robert Bernasconi, "Fanon's *The Wretched of the Earth* as Fulfillment of Sartre's *Critique of Dialectical Reason*," *Sartre Studies International* 16, no. 2 (2010): 36.

12 Jean-Paul Sartre, *Critique of Dialectical Reason Volume One*, trans. Alan Sheridan-Smith (London: Verso, 2004), 20.

13 Sartre, *Critique*, 803.

14 Bernasconi, "Fanon's *The Wretched of the Earth*," 44.

SECTION 2
IDEAS

MODULE 5
MAIN IDEAS

KEY POINTS

- The themes in *The Wretched of the Earth* are primarily psychological: anger because the colonized are made to feel inferior; and the need for violence as a purge for both the inferiority complex and the colonial situation that creates it.

- Fanon argues that violence alone can oust colonialism,* itself a violent institution. It cannot be destroyed either by negotiation or by change initiated by the Westernized middle classes.

- The rhetoric of *Wretched* was intended to fire the revolutionary spirit of colonized people and (according to the philosopher Jean-Paul Sartre*) to intimidate and shame European readers.

Key Themes

The main themes of Frantz Fanon's *The Wretched of the Earth* are the importance of human dignity and rights, and the psychological damage caused when these are denied in the unequal colonial relationship. Fanon's analysis of colonialism is not focused on the workshops or the fields, but on the minds of the colonized. "It is a systematic negation," Fanon says of the colonial relationship, "and a furious determination to deny the other person all attributes of humanity." The colonized must "ask themselves the question constantly:'who am I?'"[1] The colonizer knows who he is, because he is recognized as an equal or a superior by everyone around him, but the colonized person is just the "natural background to the presence of the French."[2]

> ❝ If we wish to describe [decolonization] precisely, we might find it in the well-known words: 'the last shall be first and the first last.' ❞
>
> Frantz Fanon, *The Wretched of the Earth*

One of the other critical themes of *Wretched* is class within this psychological context. Fanon believes that the colonial relationship—and, specifically, the mentality of the colonial relationship—will not end if people who have achieved high social status under European rule achieve power. This is because they have answered the question "who am I?" with the answer "European." The rural peasantry, on the other hand, are still confronted with the same question and have neither the means nor the desire to make themselves European. Fanon's solution is both psychological and political: violent revolution not only destroys the colonial state, but brings the catharsis* (roughly, a purging) of colonial rage felt by those whose humanity has been systematically denied.

Exploring the Ideas

One of the first premises of Fanon's work is violence: "decolonization is always a violent phenomenon."[3] Why is this? Fanon says it is because the colonial relationship was born in, and is sustained by, violence. The "first encounter" between the colonizer and the colonized, the very institution of the colonial relationship, "was marked by violence." Fanon writes that "the exploitation of the native by the settler" was carried "by dint of a great array of bayonets and cannon."[4] From this point on, the relationship is on the settler's terms and he or she holds all the power. However, the colonized person, of course, is a human being, and therefore entitled to rights and dignity. Even more importantly, he or she knows this and so the disparity between that person's natural rights and his or her inferior treatment produces first

35

anger, and eventually violence. For Fanon, this means that the "narrow world [of colonialism], strewn with prohibitions" and sustained by violence, "can only be called in question by absolute violence."[5]

In this sense, Fanon's conception of the colonial world cannot accept compromise or settlement. It is too Manichean*—meaning it sees the world in terms of opposing forces of absolute right and wrong. Without the complete destruction of the colonial world, Fanon believes, nothing can be achieved. There is another reason nonviolence cannot work. It is because "the colonies have become a market" for capitalist* goods from the mother country.[6] With an agreed handover to native rule, capitalists (those who profit from investment and the labor of others) essentially expect that little will change, and the colonial country will become a new country in name only. "Out of the conference … comes the political selectiveness which enables Monsieur M'ba,* the president of the Republic of Gabon," to be officially recognized by France as the head of a nominally independent state. There is, though, no real difference in the status quo and the change is one merely of symbolic political theater.[7]

Who, then, must carry out this violent revolution? Fanon uses the Marxist* term "lumpenproletariat,"* meaning the very lowest rung of society; these are people often living in urban slums or in the countryside, a "horde of starving men" that "constitutes one of the most spontaneous and the most radically revolutionary forces of a colonized people."[8]

The colonized middle class, on the other hand, cannot be an effective spearhead, and would not make effective postcolonial rulers. "In its willful narcissism,"* Fanon writes, "the national middle class is easily convinced" that it can step in and take over the country. However, its habit of dependence on the settler class for its status and its relative inexperience mean it will "send out frenzied appeals for help to the former mother country."[9] In effect, the colonial middle class is simply not new, different, or radical enough to overturn colonialism. Otherwise, "there's nothing save a minimum of readaptation, a few reforms at the top, a flag waving: and down there at the bottom," meaning the lumpenproletariat, "an undivided mass, still living in the Middle Ages."[10]

Language and Expression

Fanon wrote *Wretched* rhetorically.* The book was not intended, in the words of the US historian Edmund Burke III,* to be a "scholarly autopsy," but was, rather, a "call to arms."[11] Fanon does not urge his audience to take a calm, rational tone with colonial authorities. "The natives' challenge to the colonial world is not a rational confrontation of points of view," but is instead, "the untidy affirmation" of the idea that this state of affairs must end.[12]

Ultimately, *Wretched* was written not out of criticism, but out of anger. In the introduction to the book, Jean-Paul Sartre writes of Fanon that he, "an ex-native, French speaking, bends [the French language of the colonizer] to new requirements, makes use of it, and speaks to the colonized only."[13] But, Sartre goes on, there is something to be gained from the fiery writing for Europeans: "you [the European reader], who are so liberal and so humane … you pretend to forget that you own colonies and that in them men are massacred in your name."[14] Readers from colonizing nations, he suggests, should be made to feel ashamed and threatened by this book.

NOTES

1 Frantz Fanon, *The Wretched of the Earth*, trans. Constance Farrington (London: Penguin, 2001), 200.

2 Fanon, *Wretched*, 201.

3 Fanon, *Wretched*, 27.

4 Fanon, *Wretched*, 28.

5 Fanon, *Wretched*, 29.

6   Fanon, *Wretched*, 51.

7   Fanon, *Wretched*, 52.

8   Fanon, *Wretched*, 103.

9   Fanon, *Wretched*, 120.

10 Fanon *Wretched*, 118.

11 Edmund Burke III, "Frantz Fanon's 'The Wretched of the Earth'," *Daedalus* 105, no. 1 (1976): 129.

12 Fanon, *Wretched*, 31.

13 Jean-Paul Sartre, "Introduction," in Fanon, *Wretched*, 9.

14 Sartre, in Fanon, *Wretched*, 12.

MODULE 6
SECONDARY IDEAS

KEY POINTS

- Fanon is equally concerned with the individual's potential for psychological liberation in the aftermath of violent, cathartic* revolution (that is, an experience in which negative feelings associated with domination are purged) as with the revolution itself.

- National culture will be rebuilt through violence as the colonized recover their humanity—but while nationalist* sentiment (the belief that defining oneself as part of a particular nation is of primary importance) has the potential to bind revolutionaries together, it may hamper the formation of a cohesive state.

- *The Wretched of the Earth* contains medical case studies, illustrating the link between colonial rule and mental illness.

Other Ideas

While Frantz Fanon's *The Wretched of the Earth* focuses primarily on inciting revolution, he also has much to say on what happens afterward. What does Fanon see happening psychologically to people, to the national culture, and the new government? The most important thing, for Fanon, is that the people of the new nation neither "imitate Europe" nor concern themselves with "[catching] up to Europe."[1] His rhetoric*—his skill with persuasive language—is powerful and historical: decolonization* "is a question of the Third World* starting a new history of Man," one that does not "pay tribute to Europe" but invents new forms of social organization.[2]

❝ The economic channels of the young state sink back inevitably into neo-colonialist lines. The national economy, formerly protected, is today literally controlled. The budget is balanced through loans and gifts, while every three or four months the chief ministers ... come to the erstwhile mother countries or elsewhere, fishing for capital. ❞

Frantz Fanon, *The Wretched of the Earth*

This leads Fanon to recap his critique of the native middle class. "Bourgeois* [middle class] nationalist anticolonialism," writes the commentator on colonialism Neil Lazarus,* merely aims to supplant the colonizers, and leads to a state that is equally corrupt and exploitative, and trapped in the thrall of its "mother country."[3] Nationalism, Fanon believes, is the common identity of the colonized people, binding them in a common struggle. Ultimately, however, he argues that nationalism must transform from a sentiment of pride and shared identity into a common project (he called this "national consciousness") in order to build a functioning state.

Exploring the Ideas

What is achieved through the violent eradication of a colonial society? Most importantly, the colonized individual reclaims his (or her) own humanity: "he finds his freedom in and through violence."[4] Fanon writes that violence is inherently cathartic (that is, purgative) for the colonized subject: "it frees the native from his inferiority complex," and the consciousness of the people *as a people* (rather than as a problem, a servant, or a subjugated being) is awakened.[5]

Colonized people are, in this sense, being freed from dehumanization: "The terms the settler uses when he mentions the native are zoological terms," but the colonized person "knows that he is not an animal; and it is precisely at the moment he realizes his humanity that he begins to sharpen the weapons with which he will secure its victory."[6] The great hope of restoring his human dignity means the violence of the colonized man is "positive and creative," and "introduces into each man's consciousness the idea of a common cause." That cause is the creation of a nation, and means that the revolutionaries are participating in a historical act.[7]

The act of nation-building on the part of the revolutionaries is critical. It is in the interest of the colonizer, argues Fanon, to claim that the colony was not a "nation" before the Europeans arrived, and that, if the Europeans left, it would descend into chaos.[8] One of the key tasks is reclaiming the culture of the nation, and building it through revolution; it is not only the music, stories, and other cultural artifacts *of the past*, but also *of the ongoing struggle*. That is, "the national Algerian culture is taking on form and content as the battles are being fought" against the French.[9]

While national culture may be important, Fanon is skeptical about nationalism. He believes that newly independent states run the risk of being captured by their leaders, meaning the lives of the "lumpenproletariat"* would be no better than they were during colonialism. Leaders build a strong police force and army. "By dint of yearly loans," the state props itself up, "scandals are numerous, ministers grow rich ... and there is not a soul ... who does not join in the great procession of corruption," and rely on nationalist rhetoric to stay in power.[10] Fanon writes that national consciousness must quickly evolve "a consciousness of social and political needs," including maintaining an army that is loyal to the state (rather than its generals), well-educated youth, and inclusive economic policies.[11]

Nationalism, for Fanon, is a useful stepping-stone, but it can ultimately be damaging and must be replaced by a genuine consciousness of social and political needs, rather than the hollow glorification of a nation.

41

Overlooked

Most of the academic focus on *Wretched* involves its earlier chapters, especially "On Violence." The medical historian Richard Keller,* however, is more interested in the later chapters, where Fanon, a psychiatrist by profession, reports case studies of patients he saw under colonial rule. "If *Wretched* is a diatribe against colonial violence," Keller writes, "it is one extrapolated from the empirical experience of treating patients rendered dysfunctional by a violent social order."[12] Fanon believes that these case studies are important, and the unique effect of colonialism on the psyche has been ignored: "After two great world wars," he writes, "there is no lack of publications on the mental pathology" of those involved, but the "colonial war" is different and gives rise to new and overlooked conditions.[13]

One of the case studies, for example, investigates the murder of a European boy by two Algerian peers. All were in their early teens. "He was a good friend of ours," said one of the boys to Fanon, but "one day we decided to kill him, because the Europeans want to kill all the Arabs." Deciding they could not manage to kill an adult European, they contented themselves with their friend.[14] Another case study examined a French police interrogator who had tortured Algerian revolutionaries, and suffered a mental breakdown as a result. "This man knew perfectly well that his disorders were directly caused by the kind of activity that went on inside the rooms where interrogations were carried out," wrote Fanon, but "he could not see his way to stopping," as it would cost him his job.[15] Ultimately, the final chapters, as Keller writes, uncover "the link between madness and colonial violence."[16]

NOTES

1   Frantz Fanon, *The Wretched of the Earth*, trans. Constance Farrington (London: Penguin, 2001), 252.

2   Fanon, *Wretched*, 254.

3   Neil Lazarus, "Disavowing Decolonization: Fanon, Nationalism, and the Problematic of Representation in Current Theories of Colonial Discourse," *Research in African Literatures* 24, no. 4 (1993): 71.

4   Fanon, *Wretched*, 68.

5   Fanon, *Wretched*, 74.

6   Fanon, *Wretched*, 33.

7   Fanon, *Wretched*, 73.

8   Fanon, *Wretched*, 169.

9   Fanon, *Wretched*, 187.

10 Fanon, *Wretched*, 138.

11 Fanon, *Wretched*, 164.

12 Richard C. Keller, "Clinician and Revolutionary: Frantz Fanon, Biography, and the History of Colonial Medicine," *Bulletin of the History of Medicine* 81, no. 4 (2007): 837–8.

13 Fanon, *Wretched*, 202.

14 Fanon, *Wretched*, 217–18.

15 Fanon, *Wretched*, 215–17.

16 Keller, "Clinician and Revolutionary," 830.

MODULE 7
ACHIEVEMENT

KEY POINTS

- *The Wretched of the Earth* influenced numerous revolutionary movements, but has been criticized as overreliant on an "idealized" image of peasants.

- The book influenced counterculture movements in South Africa, Iran, the United States, and around the world, despite being banned in France.

- Feminists* (those actively engaged in the struggle for equality between the sexes) debate whether Fanon has a "blind spot" as far as gender is concerned.

Assessing the Argument

Frantz Fanon's *The Wretched of the Earth* was to be considered a singularly important text in the global struggle to end colonial domination—it has been called the "bible of decolonization"* by the cultural theorist Stuart Hall.*[1] Fanon himself would consider the book a success, as it incited real action. He did not consider himself a theorist as much as an actor in the global struggle against colonialism.* In the United States, for example, *Wretched* became the "bible" of the radical black nationalist Black Panther* movement ("One day," said Black Panther Bobby Seale,* "I went over to [founding member Huey P. Newton's*] house and asked him if he had read Fanon … I knew Fanon was right"). For people such as Seale, the question became how to get Fanon's ideas out into the world.[2] Fanon achieved his goal because he inspired revolutionaries around the world.

On another level, however, Fanon's theoretical model depends on an image of Algerian peasants (and peasants in general) that Mohamed

> " Huey understood the meaning of what Fanon was saying about organizing the lumpenproletariat first … organizing the brother who's pimping, the brother who's hustling, the unemployed, the downtrodden, the brother who's robbing banks, who's not politically conscious, 'that's what lumpenproletariat means' that if you didn't relate to these cats, the power structure would organize these cats against you. "
>
> Bobby Seale, *Seize the Time*

Harbi,* an Algerian and fellow partisan of the Algerian liberation organization *Front de Libération Nationale* (FLN),* described as somewhat nostalgic. The peasants were fragmented across countries, fighting for survival rather than identity.[3] Fanon's argument was less important, however, for what it said about Algeria in particular, than the extent to which it helped direct the global anticolonial revolution.

Achievement in Context

In 1960, the United Nations* accelerated the call for decolonization, requiring, among other things, complete and immediate self-determination for colonized countries, regardless of their perceived readiness for self-determination.[4] This process was part of a growing, and increasingly intense, demand for emancipation (freedom) around the world, and *Wretched*, first translated from French to English in 1963, helped fuel it.

It has been noted that it was not only the Black Panthers who turned to *Wretched*; in the early 1970s, Steve Biko,* an activist in the struggle for the liberation of black South Africans, circulated *Wretched* among the South African Students Organization* where it became "the center of the black consciousness movement."[5] In an Irish prison

45

cell, Bobby Sands* of the Provisional Irish Republican Army (Provisional IRA),* a paramilitary group in Ireland that aimed to overthrow British sovereignty in Northern Ireland, was "set alight" by Fanon's rhetoric. The Iranian intellectual Ali Shariati* translated *Wretched* into Farsi, and "in the early days of the Iranian Revolution* posters bearing Fanon's image" appeared.[6] These few are an indicative, rather than an exhaustive, list of revolutionary movements influenced by Fanon.

When Fanon died, the police seized copies of *Wretched* from shelves in France, but as the English historian David Macey* writes, representatives of the Provisional Government of Algeria at the UN "gave copies … to diplomats as Christmas presents."[7] Fanon's book appeared at a critical moment for liberation movements around the world; it was seen as profoundly dangerous and countercultural by the powers-that-be.

Limitations

Fanon has been accused of having a "blind spot" when it comes to the issue of women in colonial society, particularly in Algeria. The Indian scholar Ketu Katrak* notes that Fanon "does not analyze the double oppression—racist and sexist—of the colonized woman."[8] Referencing "patriarchy,"* a set of social arrangements where males, or things considered to be masculine, are favored, Katrak notes that the "colonized woman" struggles against both the racist colonial society and the patriarchal attitudes of her own society.[9] In other words, Fanon's analysis was limited—for Katrak—because the problem of patriarchy is, if it is considered at all, simply a subproblem of colonialism.

The feminist thinker Tracy Denean Sharpley-Whiting* offers a response to feminist critics of Fanon. She argues that accusing Fanon of having a gender "blind spot" misses the point of his analysis. She says that, rather than evaluating whether to think of Fanon as feminist, "it is perhaps more appropriate … to speak of Fanon's radically humanist profeminist consciousness."[10] She thinks Fanon's work should be seen as more *generally* emancipatory. This makes it entirely compatible with feminism, even if it is not overtly feminist (hence, the phrase "profeminist" rather than "feminist").

NOTES

1   Stuart Hall, quoted in Homi Bhabha, "Foreword: Framing Fanon," in *The Wretched of the Earth* by Frantz Fanon, trans. Richard Philcox (New York: Grove Press, 2004), XVI.

2   Bobby Seale, *Seize the Time: The Story of the Black Panther Party and Huey P. Newton* (Baltimore, MD: Black Classic Press, 1991), 25.

3   Mohamed Harbi, quoted in David Macey, *Frantz Fanon: A Biography* (London: Verso, 2012), 481.

4   United Nations, *Declaration on the Granting of Independence to Colonial Countries and Peoples*, December 14, 1960, accessed October 3, 2015, www.un.org/en/decolonization/declaration.shtml.

5   Bhabha, "Foreword," *Wretched* (2004), XXVIII.

6   Alice Cherki, *Frantz Fanon: A Portrait*, trans. Nadia Benabid (Ithaca, NY: Cornell University Press, 2006), 200.

7   Macey, *Frantz Fanon*, 487.

8   Ketu Katrak, "Decolonizing Culture: Toward a Theory for Postcolonial Women's Texts," *MFS Modern Fiction Studies* 35, no. 1 (1989): 162.

9   Katrak, "Decolonizing Culture," 162.

10 Tracy Denean Sharpley-Whiting, *Frantz Fanon: Conflicts and Feminisms* (Lanham, MD: Rowman and Littlefield, 1998), 24.

PLACE IN THE AUTHOR'S WORK

KEY POINTS

- Fanon was a prolific writer and his books are generally collections or expansions of articles written for radical French magazines.

- In *The Wretched of the Earth*, Fanon's thinking shifted away from analyzing the psychology of race relations to calling for revolution.

- *Wretched* remains a significant work, as do Fanon's other writings, but it remains up for debate whether or not his ideas should be seen as independent of his own particular situation.

Positioning

Frantz Fanon, the author of *The Wretched of the Earth*, published four major books, as well as numerous articles. His first book, *Black Skin, White Masks* (1952), began its life as his doctoral dissertation at the University of Lyon, "Essay for the Disalienation of the Black." It was published before Fanon moved to Algeria and, while it catapulted him into Parisian intellectual circles, it was not widely read until after his death.[1] Following the book's publication, however, Fanon began working as a psychiatrist and started to write psychiatric technical papers prolifically, coauthoring three in the first month of his career.[2]

In 1953, Fanon moved to Algeria. The beginning of the Algerian War* in 1954, in which Algerians fought for independence from colonial France, marked a stark break in his career: he went from being a theorist on racial psychiatry to advocating a violent praxis* (turning ideas into action). His subsequent work demonstrates this shift in

> **❝** As for us, we have long since rehabilitated the Algerian colonized man. We have wrenched the Algerian man from a centuries-old and implacable oppression. We have risen to our feet and we are now moving forward. Who can settle us back in servitude? **❞**
>
> Frantz Fanon, *A Dying Colonialism (L'an V de la révolution Algérienne)*

thought. In 1959, he published *L'an V de la révolution Algérienne* ("The Fifth Year of the Algerian Revolution"; the English version was titled *A Dying Colonialism*). This book focused mainly on Algeria, rather than the colonial system in general, but contained plenty of universal messages about liberation and total revolution. The rejection of gradual change is especially telling with regard to the shift from racial theorizing to revolutionary advocacy. Fanon says the "launching of a new society is possible only within the framework of national independence," meaning all theorizing and all change can occur only after the colonial society is destroyed.[3]

The Wretched of the Earth was written between 1960 and 1961, though its most famous chapter, "Concerning Violence," was published separately beforehand. *Toward the African Revolution* appeared after Fanon's death and consisted of a collection of his articles, previously published in *El Moujahid* (a revolutionary magazine in Algeria), and left-wing magazines in France such as *Esprit* and *Les Temps modernes*.

Integration

The theme of the power of revolution to transform the individual— to help him or her shed the inferiority complex Fanon analyzed in his earlier career—was critical in his later work. His early output had fought a battle within the psyche of the colonized. Fanon wrote *Black Skin, White Masks* as a psychological treatise to "help the black man to free himself of the arsenal of complexes that has been developed by the colonial environment."[4] The book deals with the psychology that forces black people to choose between either being black and so considering themselves inferior, or Europeanizing themselves, and accepting the view that holds blackness to be inferior. His article "West Indians and Africans" talks about the moment where Fanon turned from a "West Indian"—according to Fanon, a Caribbean who does not think of himself as particularly "black," "[identifying] himself with the white man"—into a black man.[5] Fanon felt that his own "white mask" had been torn off by European racists, who from their viewpoint of cultural authority regarded West Indians and Africans to be the same.

In the shadow of the Algerian War, Fanon's writing changed. He became less concerned with discussing the relationship between Europeans and black people as a problem of inferiority and identity, and more interested in examining the drive for dignity among the colonized. For example, in "Letter to the Resident Minister" (his official resignation from the psychiatric hospital in the Algerian city of Blida), published in 1956, Fanon wrote that the revolution was the result of the "fundamental aspiration to dignity" of the Algerian people.[6] "The power of the Algerian Revolution," Fanon wrote in *A Dying Colonialism*, "henceforth resides in the radical mutation that the Algerian has undergone."[7]

Significance

"When Frantz Fanon died in December 1961," writes the professor of African studies Emmanuel Hansen,* "he was relatively unknown," except among those directly involved in Algeria, and "a small group of French Leftists who had been attracted to his writings."[8] While he was alive and publishing articles that decried French colonialism in Algeria, numerous attempts were made on his life, because his work was considered so intellectually dangerous.[9] By the 1970s, however, Frantz Fanon had become a household name.

Along with his fame, an academic discipline emerged, embracing not only the development of Fanon's postcolonial* project, but also the study of his writing ("Fanon studies"). The historian Henry Louis Gates, Jr.* writes that those who engage in "Fanon studies" must take care, however, not to turn Fanon into a kind of "concept"—"a transcultural, transhistorical Global Theorist," given his legendary status as the most strident early postcolonialist. Students of Fanon should instead focus on "reading him," rather than mythologizing him, and remember "his own historical particularity," as someone from a particular time and place who dealt with concrete situations—rather than as a transcendent intellectual force, divorced from the real world.[10]

NOTES

1   Ziauddin Sardard, "Introduction," in *Black Skin, White Masks* by Frantz Fanon, trans. Charles Lam Markmann (London: Pluto Press, 2008), ix.

2   David Macey, *Frantz Fanon: A Biography* (London: Verso, 2012), 198.

3   Frantz Fanon, *A Dying Colonialism*, trans. Haakon Chevalier (New York: Grove Press, 1965), 179.

4   Fanon, *Black Skin, White Masks*, 19.

5   Fanon, "West Indians and Africans," in *Toward the African Revolution*, trans. Haakon Chevalier (New York: Grove Press, 1965), 26.

6   Fanon, "Letter to the Resident Minister," in *Toward the African Revolution*, 53.

7   Fanon, *A Dying Colonialism*, 33.

8   Emmanuel Hansen, "Frantz Fanon: Portrait of a Revolutionary Intellectual," *Transition* 46 (1974): 25.

9   Hansen, "Frantz Fanon," 34.

10 Henry Louis Gates, Jr., "Critical Fanonism," *Critical Inquiry* 17, no. 3 (1991): 471.

SECTION 3
IMPACT

MODULE 9
THE FIRST RESPONSES

KEY POINTS

- The *Wretched of the Earth* was criticized for claiming violence is politically legitimate.
- While Fanon died before he could respond, others have suggested that this is a misunderstanding of his argument.
- In the course of time, the debates over Fanon became less concerned with violence, and more interested in how to appropriate him in new contexts.

Criticism

On its publication, Frantz Fanon's *The Wretched of the Earth* invited serious criticism. One strand of criticism came from Marxists,* who argued that Fanon was insufficiently Marxist, given that he dismisses the idea that an intellectual urban vanguard could lead African peasants to victory. Fanon did not trust the colonized middle class—a dismissal that, contrary to Marxist ideas, rules out a significant portion of the possible actors in any revolutionary struggle.[1]

The most powerful criticism of *Wretched* came from the German American political theorist Hannah Arendt,* who abhorred Fanon's endorsement of violence (though she is even more horrified with Jean-Paul Sartre's* introduction, which goes further). Intellectuals in Europe, according to Arendt, were beginning to feel "revulsion against violence in all its forms." She pointed to the successes of nonviolence in bringing about victories in the US Civil Rights Movement* (the broad struggle for equality for the black citizens of the United States) and so was dismayed by this emerging "extremism," and the glorification of violence.[2] The real problem, though, was that Fanon

> **"** Power is indeed of the essence of all government, but violence is not. Violence is by nature instrumental; like all means, it always stands in need of guidance and justification through the end it pursues. And what needs justification through something else cannot be the essence of anything. **"**
>
> Hannah Arendt, "Reflections on Violence"

and his supporters (namely Sartre) glorified violence for its own sake. It was not a *necessary evil* merely to remove the French from Algeria (for example), but rather a therapeutic, inherently dignified action. In other words, for Fanon, violence is both *justified* and *legitimate*: it is made necessary by circumstances, but it is also *the right thing to do*.

Arendt believes politics is about life and creation: "the political" occurs when human beings come together to invent something new. The US Declaration of Independence,* for instance—the founding document of the United States in which 13 of Great Britain's American colonies declared themselves independent—came about by people getting together and sharing ideas. The violence involved was necessary, but it existed only in order to make space for the *political aspect* of American independence, which was not violent. The violence, in other words, was incidental to the real project.[3] Arendt's criticism of Fanon is that violence is anything but incidental in his anticolonial theory, meaning that the political project will become conflated with the regrettable means used to achieve it. Violence and politics, she argues, are not the same thing.

Responses

The literature and language scholar Homi Bhabha* of Harvard argues that "Arendt's objection to *The Wretched of the Earth* has less to do with the occurrence of violence" than with "Fanon's teleological* belief."[4] In other words, for Bhabha, Arendt is not objecting to violence, as much as the idea that violence *is destined to occur* and will lead to a better world.

Bhabha has an alternative view of what Fanon meant by violence, as "part of a struggle for psycho-affective survival"—the survival of identity and action—and "a search for human agency in the midst of the agony of oppression."[5] The colonized is made to feel inferior by the colonizer, but does not believe that he (or she) is inferior; he is simply forced to act that way through threat of violence ("life in death" or "continued agony"). He is, in this sense, *dominated*, but not *domesticated*, and his willingness to live under such torture becomes fainter and fainter. At this point, the tension leading to violence between the colonizer and colonized is not seen merely as the "political cause" of a nation, to which Arendt objected, but "a psychic and affective curse" of an individual[6]—a curse, roughly, of the mind, person, and consciousness.

Conflict and Consensus

The Algerian War* was Fanon's primary subject in *Wretched*. The outcome of that war, though, revealed how violent revolution did not fulfill Fanon's goals. It is open to question whether post-independence Algeria has developed in a way Fanon might consider either positive or revolutionary.[7] In the aftermath of the revolution, "the masses" who had been humiliated and deprived under the colonial regime found their position little improved. The new state took over French economic interests such as the mines and factories, and so on, but this had limited impact on their emancipation.[8] This failure to bring about mass emancipation is connected to another of Fanon's concerns—the failure of nationalism* to achieve political change for anyone other than a minority elite connected directly to the new state.

Fanon's role in this debate is twofold. First, do Fanon's ideas work in today's globalized world? "It is no secret," the French Algerian psychologist Alice Cherki* writes, "that economic globalization* today is creating a greater inequality not only between North and South but also within Western societies," and that losers are relegated to "subhuman" lives.[9] Whether or not we can take Fanon from his "historical subjectivity"—his real experiences in the direct colonialism of 1950s Algeria—and apply him to the indirect neocolonialism* of the late twentieth and early twenty-first centuries is the second debate.

Ultimately, as the historian Henry Louis Gates, Jr.* writes in "Critical Fanonism," the question has become less about debating such matters as the role of violence in *Wretched* and more about claiming Fanon as the inspiration for various postcolonial* projects. "Frantz Fanon," Gates writes, "not to put too fine a point on it, is a Rorschach blot with legs."[10] What he means by this is that Fanon has, in some ways, become an ink-blot test: simply something onto which commentators can project their own ideas and preoccupations.

NOTES

1 Nguyen Nghe, paraphrased in L. Adele Jinadu, *Fanon: In Search of the African Revolution* (London: KPI, 1986), 115.

2 Hannah Arendt, "A Special Supplement: Reflections on Violence," *New York Review of Books*, February 27, 1969, accessed October 4, 2015, www.nybooks.com/articles/archives/1969/feb/27/a-special-supplement-reflections-on-violence/.

3 Hannah Arendt, *On Violence* (New York: Harcourt Brace, 1969), 79.

4 Homi Bhabha, "Foreword: Framing Fanon," in *The Wretched of the Earth* by Frantz Fanon, trans. Richard Philcox (New York: Grove Press, 2004), xxxv.

5 Bhabha, "Foreword," *Wretched*, xxxvi.

6 Bhabha, "Foreword," *Wretched*, xxxix.

7 Paul A. Beckett, "Algeria vs. Fanon: The Theory of Revolutionary Decolonization, and the Algerian Experience," *Western Political Quarterly* 26, no. 1 (1973): 6.

8   Beckett, "Algeria vs. Fanon," 25–6.

9   Alice Cherki, *Frantz Fanon: A Portrait*, trans. Nadia Benabid (Ithaca, NY: Cornell University Press, 2006), 221.

10 Henry Louis Gates, Jr., "Critical Fanonism," *Critical Inquiry* 17, no. 3 (1991): 458.

MODULE 10
THE EVOLVING DEBATE

KEY POINTS

- As postcolonialism,* a discipline that deals with the various legacies of colonialism,* has become increasingly allied with the analytical approach of poststructuralism,* it has become more concerned with distinctively poststructuralist concerns such as colonialism's influence on representation and the production of knowledge.

- *The Empire Writes Back* (1989) is an excellent statement of postcolonial theory, with a central focus on the "binaries" (good/evil, white/black, civilized/savage) that perpetuate the colonial system.

- The poststructuralist scholar Homi Bhabha's* theory of hybridity is heavily influenced by Fanon, but focuses on the ways in which colonialism produces *new kinds* of people, rather than producing clashes of fixed identities.

Uses and Problems

We may consider Frantz Fanon's *The Wretched of the Earth* to be an early example of postcolonialist thought. Postcolonialism is an analytical approach to the various cultural, social, and psychological legacies of colonialism, famously exemplified by the Palestinian American thinker Edward Said's* 1978 book *Orientalism*. Said's work locates the problem of colonialism not in domination, but in *representation*—literary and scholarly description, say, or characters in films—that reinforces the colonized person's feelings of inferiority by making him or her an object to be managed.

In classical representations of foreigners in European art and literature, Said writes, "The Orient appears [as] a system of

> " As much as the West itself, the Orient is an idea that has a history and a tradition of thought, imagery, and vocabulary that have given it reality and presence in and for the West. "
>
> Edward Said, *Orientalism*

representations framed by a whole set of forces that brought the Orient into Western learning, Western consciousness, and later, Western empire."[1] After the colonial revolutions, "the Arab Muslim" became a figure in American culture, academia, and policy planning, understood as a force of nature or a threat to be managed "in large numbers ... [defined by] mass rage and misery," always with the "lurking threat of jihad."[2]

The implicit and powerful difference between the "orientalist" and the "oriental" is that the latter is an object of study for the former.[3] What is most important about this is that the West assumes the authority to "construct" the Orient as a threat, making it a single entity to be "handled."

An important development in postcolonialism came on its integration with the analytical approach known as poststructuralism. Poststructuralism, in brief, says that there is no such thing as "knowledge" independent of "power"; anything one can claim to "know" authoritatively (for instance, one can "know" about the Arab tendency to wage *jihad*, or holy war) is ultimately "produced" by power.[4] From here, we get the postcolonialist thinker Gayatri Spivak's* theory of the subaltern, the term she uses to refer to those who are completely powerless, such as poor, rural Indian women. Spivak believes that the subaltern is the victim of "epistemic violence." *Epistemic* refers to having and communicating ideas; since they are denied a voice in a (Western) discourse (that is, roughly, a system of language and assumptions used to discuss something) that constructs them, subalterns are subjected to violence—even if that violence exists only in the realm of ideas. To study colonial subjects, even with good intentions, even to give them a voice, "will, in the long run, cohere with the work of imperialist subject-constitution," meaning it will continue to remind the subalterns that they are lesser, silent, or marginalized.[5] Why is this? Because academic speech largely occurs between white men and white men "over here"—academics, policymakers, and so forth—representing and deciding for brown men and women "over there."

Schools of Thought

Postcolonialism has many strands—we might think of them as "critical" and "material" (this distinction is oversimplified, but is helpful for grasping the broad concerns). "Critical" postcolonial theory is mostly inspired by Fanon and is focused on "alienation and psychological marginalization," and the creation of "paired oppositions such as good–evil; true–false; white–black."[6] Postcolonial writing, exemplified by *The Empire Writes Back* (1989), tries to discover where these imagined dichotomies—false opposites—exist (especially where they reproduce the power of the colonizer states and represent Western ideas as superior), and to "interrogate European discourse ... [and] investigate the means by which Europe imposed and maintained its codes in its colonial domination of so much of the rest of the world."[7]

Just as the postcolonial project has become increasingly concerned with culture, the act of "the empire writing back" (the former colonies finding and asserting their own identities as equal to the former state) is to culture as Fanon's call for violence was to politics—but this thinking is concerned primarily with "text." Ultimately, "Fanonism" corresponds to "the sustained attempt to locate and subsequently advertise"—to figure out and then advocate—"a fixed and stable site of radical liberationist criticism and creativity."[8] This "site," in other words, is both a way of *thinking* and *living* disconnected from European domination. The "cultural hegemony"* (dominance) of Europe and the West "has been maintained" through an assumption that the formerly colonized world is composed of "isolated national offshoots" of European culture, which can be safely relegated to the margins.[9]

This does not mean, though, that postcolonial study has become concerned exclusively with poststructuralism and representation. According to one scholar, postcolonial studies should not be a matter for literary theorists concerned only with culture; they "require the analytical skills of political and social theorists, economists, historians, geographers, anthropologists, and sociologists."[10]

In Current Scholarship

The poststructuralist scholar Homi Bhabha* both responds to some of Fanon's critics and continues Fanon's project by continuing to examine the ways in which colonial relationships produce and reproduce colonial identity. He transforms Fanon's ideas, however, in very important ways. Manicheanism* (the idea of two perfectly opposed forces of good and evil, light and dark, and so on) is central to Fanon, but Bhabha moves away from this stark black-and-white confrontation and instead focuses on "hybridity." Bhabha suggests that the dividing line between the settler and the colonized is blurred, and in reality, it is difficult to specify "here" is the settler, untouched by the colonized, and "here" is the colonized, oppressed but unaltered by colonialism.[11] The colonial contact, for Bhabha, is in the everyday "crucial engagement between mask and identity, image and identification, from which comes the lasting tension of our freedom and the lasting impression of ourselves as others."[12]

What Bhabha means here is that the very fact of viewing oneself as colonized—"wearing the white mask"—has its own effect. The Manichean—black and white—picture of culture sees the colonizer and the colonized as fixed, oppositional, and located in the past; hybridity sees culture as the point of negotiation between competing demands. Bhabha uses Fanon himself as an example of hybridity: Fanon was an upper-middle-class educated doctor, working in the higher echelons of the colonial administration (as a physician at the Blida hospital), and is therefore accepted as more equal by Europeans than the everyday colonized man.[13] He is different from people who are defined by their difference. Ultimately, for Bhabha, the meeting of the colonizer and the colonized produces something entirely new.

NOTES

1   Edward Said, *Orientalism* (New York: Random House, 1994), 202–3.

2   Said, *Orientalism*, 284–5, 287.

3   Said, *Orientalism*, 308.

4   Simon Gikandi, "Poststructuralism and Postcolonial Discourse," in *The Cambridge Companion to Postcolonial Literary Studies*, ed. Neil Lazarus (Cambridge: Cambridge University Press, 2004), 98.

5   Gayatri Spivak, "Can the Subaltern Speak?" in *Marxism and the Interpretation of Culture*, ed. Cary Nelson and Lawrence Grossberg (Urbana: University of Illinois Press, 1988), 295.

6   Bill Ashcroft et al., *The Empire Writes Back: Theory and Practice in Post-Colonial Literatures* (London: Routledge, 1989), 125.

7   Ashcroft et al., *The Empire Writes Back*, 196.

8   Cedric Robinson, "The Appropriation of Frantz Fanon," *Race & Class* 35, no. 1 (1993): 88.

9   Ashcroft et al., *The Empire Writes Back*, 7.

10 Benita Parry, "The Postcolonial: Conceptual Category or Chimera?" *Yearbook of English Studies* 27 (1997): 21.

11 Homi Bhabha, "Remembering Fanon," *New Formations* 1 (1987): 122.

12 Bhabha, "Remembering Fanon," 123.

13 Homi Bhabha, *The Location of Culture* (London: Routledge, 1994), 64.

MODULE 11
IMPACT AND INFLUENCE TODAY

KEY POINTS

- Fanon is both an inspiration for postcolonialism* and a critic whose work needs little modification to show how modern "neocolonialism"* (new forms of colonialism) still denies the humanity of the lowest orders.

- From the 1990s, a rising tide of Western Islamophobia— fear of Muslims—brought about a resurgence in the kind of thinking that portrayed Africans as unable to govern. This time the idea was to make Muslims appear dangerous.

- Portraying Muslims as terrorists, according to the postcolonial academics Edward Said* and Gayatri Spivak,* is both incorrect and dangerous.

Position

Frantz Fanon's *The Wretched of the Earth* occupies a difficult space in contemporary postcolonialism.

In 1974, Guy Martin* claimed that "if one starts from the simple observation that the peasantry represents about 90% of the total African population," then those who would propose political-economic programs for Africa should start by considering their "actual" situation.[1] He was referring to the emergence of one-party states, military rule, and continued dependence on colonial powers. From this point of view, Fanon's work remains an appropriate lens through which to view the politics of struggle[2] and emancipation (freedom)—not a moment to be experienced and then consigned to the past, but rather an ongoing process.

❝ In the classical Islamic view, to which many Muslims are beginning to return, the world and all mankind are divided into two: the House of Islam, where the Muslim law and faith prevail, and the rest, known as the House of Unbelief or the House of War, which it is the duty of Muslims ultimately to bring to Islam. **❞**

Bernard Lewis, "The Roots of Muslim Rage"

"What could Frantz Fanon possibly say to Africa at this moment when the revolutionary presuppositions are apparently off the table?" asks the English social reformer Nigel C. Gibson* in his 2005 essay "Is Fanon Relevant?"[3] Our concerns, he says, are for "the dominant World Bank* 'pro-poor' rhetoric* and the postcolonial discourses," such as those of the thinkers Gayatri Spivak and Homi Bhabha,* "concerned with [hybridity] and cosmopolitan identities."[4]

In fact, the English postcolonialist scholar Neil Lazarus* suggests that poststructuralists "claiming" Fanon as an early inspiration may be misreading him. In his essay "Disavowing Decolonization," Lazarus argues that Homi Bhabha (in particular) forgets that Fanon was not only a theorist of the psychology of colonization, but had a genuine political aim, and that Bhabha falsely proposed "a vision of Fanon as preeminently a theorist of 'the colonial condition.'"[5] Bhabha, Lazarus argues, entirely ignores the fact that Fanon had a genuine picture of history, politics, and national liberation that combined with his theories of colonial identity.[6]

The Kenyan-born scholar Abdul JanMohamed* argues that examining colonialism on a purely theoretical level neglects the genuine suffering of the colonized. He uses the example of the British introduction of capitalist* agriculture to Kenya. He claims this destroyed an entire way of life for native Kenyans and to make such a historical event merely an issue about identities (focusing on "colonial discourse* as if it existed in a vacuum"[7]) ignores the fact that the Europeans "disrupted a material and discursive universe." In effect, this means that *Wretched*'s position in scholarship is up for debate: is Fanon a theorist of identity, whose ideas about colonial violence and national liberation are incidental, or is Fanon a revolutionary?

Interaction

For the French Cameroonian philosopher Achille Mbembe,* *Wretched* was an inspiration for his sustained criticism of the postcolonial world—specifically its failure to deliver on its promise of a better life for the worst off. "Surveying the post-colony, Fanon could only see a coming nightmare," Mbembe writes, as the ruling class spends large sums of money on living in luxury and "new forms of colonial warfare" that allow the West to continue occupying the developing world.[8]

He considers the relationship between Israel and Palestine, arguing, first, that the Israeli–Palestinian conflict is characterized by a "Fanonian" separation of the colonizer (the Israelis) and the colonized (the Palestinians). Even in terms of transport, the Palestinians are relegated to "dust roads," while highways connect Israeli settlements.[9] This is connected to what Mbembe calls "necropolitics," which means those in authority decide which lives matter and which are disposable.[10] The "new" colonialism is as violent as the old—"daily life is militarized," and the colonizer routinely subjects the colonized to violence.[11] In order to understand the reasons for retaliatory suicide bombing, Mbembe turns to the cultural theorist Paul Gilroy* and sees "a positive preference for death rather than continued servitude."[12] For Mbembe, then, the death of the suicide bomber is akin to the violence of the Algerian revolutionary: it is the assertion of freedom and dignity over the new colonial "necropolitics."

The Continuing Debate

From the 1990s to the present day, people—especially Muslims—who resisted this kind of occupation became portrayed as threatening, and the notion developed of a "clash of civilizations." "The Roots of Muslim Rage," an essay by the orientalist Bernard Lewis,* can be seen as an example of this kind of Islamophobia—literature that ascribes violence to Muslims. "The Muslim," writes Lewis, "has suffered successive stages of defeat. The first was his loss of domination in the world" to Europe and Russia, as well as the Westernization of his countries both economically and culturally, and the "challenge to his mastery in his own house, from emancipated women and rebellious children."[13] Therefore, the differences between "Muslims" are eradicated, and the West uses its privileged position to decide that, as an entire people, their defining characteristic is "rage."

The Clash of Civilizations by the political theorist Samuel Huntington* suggests that beliefs inherent in the Muslim and the Western worlds will lead them to inevitable conflict. Huntington argues that these future wars are likely to emerge from cultural attitudes, namely "Western arrogance, Islamic intolerance, and Sinic [Chinese] assertiveness."[14] These factors make such events as the terrorist attack on America on September 11, 2001 ("9/11"*) and the "war on terror" that followed seem (retrospectively) inevitable.

In her speech "Terror," the Columbia professor Gayatri Spivak declared that the war on terror "is part of an alibi every imperialism* has given itself, a civilizing mission carried to the extreme, as it always must be."[15] The Muslim is portrayed as a potential suicide bomber, and the Muslim woman as oppressed, so the West once again intervenes to "civilize" and "make the world safe." The Iraq War* of 2003, fought by the United States and its allies against Iraq on the grounds that the nation was stockpiling "weapons of mass destruction," and justified by this theory of Muslims as violent and backward, "demonstrates how the language of the colonizer is organized so as to 'prove' the subordinate status of the colonized."[16]

NOTES

1   Guy Martin, "Fanon's Relevance to Contemporary African Political Thought," *Ufahamu: A Journal of African Studies* 4, no. 3 (1974): 13.

2   Martin, "Fanon's Relevance," 25–9.

3   Nigel Gibson, "Is Fanon Relevant? Toward an Alternative Foreword to 'The Damned of the Earth,'" *Human Architecture* 5, no. 3 (2007): 41.

4   Gibson, "Is Fanon Relevant?," 41.

5   Neil Lazarus, "Disavowing Decolonization: Fanon, Nationalism, and the Problematic of Representation in Current Theories of Colonial Discourse," *Research in African Literatures* 24, no. 4 (1993): 88.

6   Lazarus, "Disavowing Decolonization," 88.

7   Abdul R. JanMohamed, "The Economy of Manichean Allegory: The Function of Racial Difference in Colonialist Literature," *Critical Inquiry* 12, no. 1 (1985): 60.

8   Achille Mbembe, "Metamorphic Thought: The Works of Frantz Fanon," *African Studies* 71, no. 1 (2012): 26.

9   Achille Mbembe, "Necropolitics," trans. Libby Meintjes, *Public Culture* 15, no. 1 (2003): 29.

10 Mbembe, "Necropolitics," 27.

11 Mbembe, "Necropolitics," 30.

12 Paul Gilroy, *The Black Atlantic: Modernity and Double Consciousness* (Cambridge, MA: Harvard University Press, 1993), 68.

13 Bernard Lewis, "The Roots of Muslim Rage," *The Atlantic* 266, no. 3 (1990): 49.

14 Samuel Huntington, *The Clash of Civilizations and the Remaking of World Order* (London: Simon and Schuster, 2002), 183.

15 Gayatri Spivak, "Terror: A Speech after 9/11," *boundary 2* 31, no. 2 (2004): 82.

16 Daniel Egan, "Frantz Fanon and the Construction of the Colonial Subject: Defining 'The Enemy' in the Iraq War," *Socialism and Democracy* 21, no. 3 (2007): 151.

MODULE 12
WHERE NEXT?

KEY POINTS

- The Arab Uprisings (Arab Spring)* of 2010–13 provide a new opportunity to think about Fanon, especially the failure of his second phase—colonial* uprising or building national consciousness.

- The Iranian American professor of literature Hamid Dabashi* continues Fanon's project, suggesting that "native informers" (who justify a new imperialism) help dehumanize Arabs and justify recolonization.

- The ideas in *The Wretched of the Earth* will remain relevant as long as there are dispossessed and dehumanized people struggling for recognition.

Potential

In late 2010, the Arab Uprisings, at first known as the Arab Spring, broke out. Frantz Fanon's ideas may not at first seem obviously applicable to these uprisings, as he wrote about the colonial situation, and these uprisings were against domestic authoritarianism—states in which the government exercises its authority at the expense of the liberty of that state's citizens. The English social reformer Nigel Gibson* argued in an interview of 2011, however, that Fanon's revolutionary humanism is still relevant because postcolonial states, notwithstanding a change of leadership, will often betray the people and fail to improve their lives.[1]

Gibson believes Fanon would recognize the Arab Uprisings and their attempts to create a new space for politics, after previous regimes had failed to bring freedom and identity to their people. He would see them as the result of the colonial liberation movement focusing too

❝ What could account for this discrepancy—outrage at criminal acts when the perpetrators are Muslims, yet complacency toward far worse acts when they are aimed against Muslims? How would one understand this systematic dehumanization of Arabs and Muslims—as beings capable only of criminal acts (when a mere handful have perpetrated them) coupled with disregard for their sufferings when millions of them are victims? ❞

Hamid Dabashi, *Brown Skin, White Masks*

much on *nationalism** instead of *social change*, or "developing national consciousness." What results is an "uncivil" state—it is not colonial, but it reproduces the colonial relationship, and is "defined by its inauthenticity, which is to say its historical discontinuity—and its oppressiveness."[2] In other words, it is not authentically national because it has merely recreated the old colonial order and maintains its authority with the same oppression. The uprisings represent the second stage of Fanon's vision of revolution—developing national consciousness—rather than the racial or identity-based violence that characterizes colonial revolution.

Future Directions

Hamid Dabashi wrote *Brown Skin, White Masks* in 2011, updating Fanon's insights in relation to the contemporary context of the American "War on Terror"* and the role of "native informers" who justify a new imperialism.[3] Dabashi thinks that intellectuals such as the Somali political activist Ayaan Hirsi Ali* or the American Lebanese scholar Fouad Ajami* act as "native informers," who preach that "imperial adventurism is good for the world, and above all for the people"—overwhelmingly Muslim—"targeted for invasion and

69

salvation" from their own barbarism and backwardness.[4] These "native informers," who call for Western powers to colonize their homelands and save them from themselves, "have taken over the work that the racist Orientalists once performed," and the colonial relationship—while it looks different from the European colonialism of previous years—is simply "more advanced ... with newer forms of domination in need of a renewed ideological language."[5]

This new ideological language is about international liberalism—a philosophy founded on ideas of liberty put into practice to forcibly "free" colonized women, for example, from bondage. Ultimately, Islam is inseparable from terrorism, and any political act that happens to be Muslim becomes a criminal act—this allows the US, Dabashi argues, to dominate and control the world's poorest by criminalizing their attempts at freedom.[6]

Summary

Frantz Fanon's *The Wretched of the Earth* is a seething indictment of colonialism and its psychological effects. The colonial relationship cuts the country in two—the settler space (clean, pleasant, civilized) and the native space (dirty, mean, savage). The colonized person is repressed and deemed inferior, but does not believe this is true. And because he or she does not believe it, that person must, through violence, assert his or her humanity and rediscover his or her true self. Fanon believes that the "middle classes"—colonized people who have acquired a comfortable position within colonial society—cannot be trusted to lead the revolution. At worst, they will actively suppress it; at best, the revolution will be incomplete because links with the mother country will remain, and any change will be insignificant. Fanon believes only the "lumpenproletariat"* have revolutionary potential—the dispossessed rural peasants (even if they have migrated to the cities) who want real, radical change. Equally important are Fanon's thoughts on how the colonial state dehumanizes and justifies its domination of the colonized, while the postcolonial* state, too, can betray its people and focus on nationalism* and the enrichment of elites. All of these ideas are pertinent today in an era of unending international war and creaking authoritarian dictators holding on to power. *The Wretched of the Earth* will remain relevant as long as there are dispossessed people who struggle for recognition.

NOTES

1   Yasser Munif, "Frantz Fanon and the Arab Uprisings: An Interview with Nigel Gibson," *Jadaliyya*, August 17, 2012, accessed October 5, 2015, www.jadaliyya.com/pages/index/6927/frantz-fanon-and-the-arab-uprisings_an-interview-w.

2   Jacqueline S. Ismael and Shereen T. Ismael, "The Arab Spring and the Uncivil State," *Arab Studies Quarterly* 35, no. 3 (2013): 233.

3   Hamid Dabashi, *Brown Skin, White Masks* (London: Pluto Press, 2011), 20.

4   Dabashi, *Brown Skin*, 26.

5   Dabashi, *Brown Skin*, 37.

6   Dabashi, *Brown Skin*, 112.

GLOSSARY

GLOSSARY OF TERMS

Algerian War: a conflict between France and various independence movements in Algeria. The conflict claimed lives in both France and Algeria, and eventually ended in Algerian independence.

Algiers School of Neuropsychiatry: a school of thought prevalent in French colonial hospitals, which suggested that North Africans were genetically inferior, and that resistance to colonialism was a form of madness.

Arab Uprisings (Arab Spring): a series of political uprisings that occurred in the Arab World between 2010 and 2013, starting with the self-immolation (setting oneself on fire) of a fruit vendor in Tunisia. For the most part they have not resulted in sustained political change and led to the Syrian civil war.

Black Panthers: a black nationalist organization in the United States. The party is widely credited with playing an important role in black liberation movements in America.

Bourgeoisie: a category in Marxist thought that refers to a particular social class. The bourgeoisie are the property-owning middle classes ("property" is used here to refer to forms of property that make money, such as factories).

Capitalism: a social and economic system characterized by free exchange among economic units such as companies, with profit-making as the main motivation.

Catharsis: a term meaning purging or cleansing, particularly of negative emotions such as rage and fear; its use in this sense dates back to the ancient Greek philosopher Aristotle's *Poetics*, in which Greek tragedy is discussed as providing a means of catharsis for its audiences.

Civil Rights Movement (1954–68/ongoing): the term used to refer to a number of related social movements in the United States demanding equality for African Americans.

Colonial discourse: language influenced by the colonial relationship.

Colonialism: a term referring to the practice whereby, from the fifteenth century, European states maintained presences in, and assumed (exploitative) political control over, non-European territories and the peoples in them.

Declaration of Independence, US (1776): the document by which the 13 colonies that would become the United States proclaimed themselves independent of Great Britain. This is considered the founding of the United States.

Decolonization: the process by which a country disengages itself from foreign power and occupation.

Discourse: both the language and assumptions drawn on in the discussion of a subject or an area of experience and the discussion shaped by that language and those assumptions.

Divine right: the belief that a certain social order—feudalism or absolute monarchy, for example—is sanctioned by God, and therefore unquestionable.

Double consciousness: a concept introduced by the American social theorist W. E. B. Du Bois emphasizing the fragmented self-image of African Americans. It refers to the division between a black person's "true self" and the self he or she must project to the world to appear acceptable to and assimilated in "white" society.

Evian Agreement (1962): the agreement between France and the Provisional Government of the Algerian Republic to end the Algerian War. While it mostly agreed the withdrawal of the French from Algeria, France also maintained certain military bases and commercial interests in the newly sovereign state.

Feminism: a political and intellectual movement founded on the belief that men and women should be treated equally, and that political, academic, or social activism is necessary to achieve this.

Feudalism: the political and economic system associated with medieval Europe, in which laboring tenants (serfs) worked and fought for landowners (nobles) in exchange for protection and the use of land.

Front de Libération Nationale (FLN): an Algerian nationalist party, set up in 1954, initially with the aim of seizing power from France. It later became the sole ruling party of Algeria, and remains the country's largest political party since pluralism was allowed in 1989.

Globalization: the process of growing interconnectedness among the people of the world, characterized by increasingly rapid and frequent travel, communications, and material exchanges.

Hegemony: a concept relating to the dominance of a group by one individual (or state); the "hegemon" is notable not only for compelling others to obey his or her rules, but for establishing the "rules of the game."

Imperialism: the philosophy and practice of "empire building"; this might be cultural, financial, or colonial.

Iranian Revolution (1979): an uprising that overthrew the Western-backed Shah of Iran and inaugurated the present-day Islamic Republic.

Iraq War (2003–11): an armed conflict initially between the state of Iraq and the United States, and later between the United States and armed insurgents. The justification for war was that the United States and its allies believed that Saddam Hussein, then leader of Iraq, was secretly building a stockpile of weapons of mass destruction.

Islamophobia: the irrational fear or hatred of Muslims.

Lumpenproletariat: a category in Marxist thought that refers to a particular social class. The lumpenproletariat is the lowest of the low classes: the peasantry or the disaffected beggars.

Manicheanism: a term denoting a relationship between two perfectly opposed forces of good and evil, light and dark, and so on.

Marxism: an approach to social sciences and the humanities rooted in the philosophy of the nineteenth-century German political philosopher Karl Marx. It holds that dialectics (two opposing forces) define history and are rooted in class. Ultimately, everything else, such as religion, politics, art, and so on, flows from a class relationship in which one group controls the means of production (tools and resources required for labor) and exploits another.

Narcissism: admiration for oneself that borders on obsession and is often delusional.

Nationalism: the strong belief that defining oneself as part of a particular nation is of primary importance, often with an attitude of superiority relative to those of other nations.

Nazi Party: a far-right political party in Germany, active between 1920 and 1945, and led by Adolf Hitler from 1921 onward. It advocated a highly racist, anti-Semitic and anti-Slav ideology that culminated in the Holocaust, the systematic attempt to eliminate all European Jews during World War II.

Négritude: a literary and social movement emphasizing a universal black identity, and resisting the assimilation of black culture into European culture.

Neocolonialism: a term referring to colonialism "by other means"—that is, by economic domination rather than political domination.

9/11: the name given to four coordinated terror attacks launched against the United States by the Islamic extremist group al-Qaeda. Four passenger airplanes were flown into targets around the country, including the World Trade Center in New York City and the Pentagon.

Patriarchy: a social system in which power is passed down the male line and in which males, or things considered to be masculine, are favored.

Phenomenology: a school of philosophy that examines experience and consciousness; existential phenomenology holds that our ideas about ourselves are the product of our lived experiences.

Postcolonialism: an academic discipline concerned with uncovering and criticizing the cultural (and political-economic) legacies of colonial rule.

Poststructuralism: an academic discipline that analyzes how outside influences condition us, especially those operating through language. One of its most important ideas is the rejection of the idea of the "objective."

Praxis: a term referring to the process by which a "theory" or "idea" is brought into reality through action.

Provisional Irish Republican Army (Provisional IRA): a paramilitary group in Ireland that aimed to overthrow British sovereignty in Northern Ireland.

Rhetoric: a term referring to a pattern of speech, artfully constructed and intended to persuade.

South African Students Organization (SASO): a group of South African university students who opposed apartheid; by 1974, nine of its leaders were imprisoned for conspiring against the state.

Teleology: a way of looking at the world that believes all events, good and bad, are moving toward a final, perfect end state.

Third World: a term often considered synonymous with "developing world." It actually refers to states, at the time of the Cold War, that were neither in the liberal-democratic "West" (the First World), nor the Communist USSR (the Second World).

United Nations: founded in 1945, an intergovernmental organization representing (nearly) every state in the world. It is the main organization administering international health, development, security, and similar programs.

Valladolid debate (1550–1): a debate in Spain convened by King Charles V to determine the appropriate course of action in dealing with Spanish rule in the Americas.

Vichy government: the name of the French government in the years 1940–4, when France was occupied by Nazi Germany; the Vichy government exercised little authority and complied entirely with the wishes of the occupiers.

War on Terror: the term commonly applied to American-led actions throughout the Middle East against non-state "terrorist" groups, including al-Qaeda. The drone campaign in Pakistan, the occupation of Afghanistan, and other covert and overt operations are rolled into this effort.

World Bank: a Washington-based international financial institution, founded in 1944, that provides loans to low-income countries. Its decisions are guided by a commitment to facilitating foreign investment and promoting trade integration.

World War II (1939–45): a six-year-long military conflict between fascist forces, led by Germany, Italy, and Japan, and non-fascist forces, led by the Soviet Union, the United Kingdom, and the United States. Taking place between 1939 and 1945, it was the deadliest war in history, with over 60 million civilian and military casualties.

PEOPLE MENTIONED IN THE TEXT

Fouad Ajami (1945–2014) was an American Lebanese scholar and public intellectual at Stanford University. He was an advocate of liberal reform of the Middle East.

Hannah Arendt (1906–75) was a German American political theorist. Her work focuses on what power means, especially for liberal society, and tries to outline a version of the "political" that relates to life and inclusion.

Aristotle (c. 384–c. 322 B.C.E.) was one of the most significant figures in ancient Greek philosophy. He wrote on numerous disciplines, including poetry, zoology, and politics, and his work has been considered authoritative and foundational throughout history.

Simone de Beauvoir (1908–86) was a French existentialist and feminist philosopher and public intellectual; her 1949 book *The Second Sex* is considered seminal in the history of feminism. She knew Fanon through her romantic relationship with Jean-Paul Sartre.

Jeremy Bentham (1748–1832) was a British philosopher and political figure. He is most famous for "utilitarianism," a philosophy that holds that the right action will produce the greatest happiness. In the profoundly Christian society of early modern Europe, this was radical.

Robert Bernasconi (b. 1950) is a British academic and professor of philosophy at Pennsylvania State University in the United States.

Homi Bhabha (b. 1949) is an Indian poststructuralist and professor of American literature and language at Harvard University. His work, while widely regarded as important, is also often considered singularly difficult to read.

Steve Biko (1946–77) was a South African anti-apartheid campaigner and founder of the Black Consciousness Movement. He is largely considered a martyr to the anti-apartheid cause.

Edmund Burke III (b. 1940) is a professor emeritus of history at the University of California at Santa Cruz, and has served as presidential chair of the Centre for World History (2003–7).

John Colin Carothers (1903–89) was a British medical doctor active in Kenya during the colonial uprising there called the Mau-Mau Rebellion (1952–60). He is notable for possibly engaging in torture, and for his opinion that non-Europeans were biologically inferior.

Bartolomé de las Casas (c. 1484–c. 1566) was a Spanish historian, monk, and social reformer. He is noteworthy as an advocate for the rights of natives in Spanish-occupied territories, which he saw firsthand prior to becoming a monk.

Aimé Césaire (1913–2008) was a Martiniquan surrealist poet and social activist, whose work focused on portraying an authentic black aesthetic.

Alice Cherki (b. 1936) is an Algerian psychologist and medical psychiatrist who still practices in France. She worked with Fanon at Blida and has written extensively on his life.

Christopher Columbus (c. 1450–c. 1506) was an Italian explorer. He is credited with "discovering" America for Europeans in 1492, though he was intending to find a sea route to India.

Hamid Dabashi (b. 1951) is an Iranian American professor of literature at Columbia University. He is also known as a prominent historian of Iran, and for his ideas leading to the creation of modern Iran.

W. E. B. Du Bois (1868–1963) was an American social theorist and reformer. He was educated at Harvard University and was the first African American to be awarded a doctorate. In addition to helping inspire the Civil Rights Movement, he also helped establish the NAACP (National Association for the Advancement of Colored People).

Henry Louis Gates, Jr. (b. 1950) is an African American historian and literary critic, focusing on African American issues.

Nigel Gibson is an English social reformer who has written extensively on Fanon.

Paul Gilroy (b. 1956) is a Guyanese British cultural theorist who is interested in the ways in which "Black British" culture is constructed.

Stuart Hall (1932–2014) was a British Jamaican cultural theorist, who studied cultural output to determine where in British culture power relations are established or destabilized.

Emmanuel Hansen (1937–87) was a Ghanaian professor of African studies. He focused on the state of postcolonial society, and how governments may fail their people.

Mohamed Harbi (b. 1933) is an Algerian historian and FLN member, though he was imprisoned shortly after the organization came to power.

Ayaan Hirsi Ali (b. 1969) is a Somali political activist. She is a vocal proponent of social reform in the Middle East and Africa, focusing on women's rights.

Samuel Huntington (1927–2008) was an American political theorist. His 1993 article (later made into a book) "The Clash of Civilizations?" earned him fame and notoriety, as it argued that wars in the post-Cold War world would be defined by cultural divisions.

Abdul JanMohamed (b. 1945) is a Kenyan-born academic who is currently professor of English at the University of California, Berkeley. He focuses on critical theory, with particular emphasis on African colonialism.

Ketu Katrak is an Indian professor of drama at the University of California, Irvine.

Richard Keller is a professor of the history of medicine. He specializes in colonial medicine, but also examines medicine on the fringes of society in the industrialized world (for example, his book *Chasing Ghosts* examines the social dimensions of the 2003 heat wave in Paris).

Neil Lazarus is a professor of comparative literature and English at Warwick University in the United Kingdom. He specializes in the literary representations of colonialism.

Vladimir Lenin (1870–1924) was a Russian politician and political theorist. As a leader of the Russian Revolution in 1917, he was the first premier of the newly formed Soviet Union.

Bernard Lewis (b. 1916) is a British orientalist and professor of Near Eastern studies at Princeton University.

David Macey (1949–2011) was an English historian of French left-wing intellectualism, and a prolific biographer (his works include the most authoritative biography of Frantz Fanon).

Octave Mannoni (1899–1989) was a French psychologist, well known for his work on colonization psychology.

Guy Martin is an academic, formerly associated with the University of Nairobi.

Karl Marx (1818–83) was a German philosopher and economist, and a significant figure in the International Workingmen's Association. He was exiled from continental Europe to London in 1849 for his radical pro-worker views. His philosophy, Marxism, remains foundational in many disciplines.

Léon M'ba (1902–67) was the first prime minister and president of Gabon (1961–7), a West African country that was formerly a French colony. He established Gabon as a one-party state in 1964 with the tacit backing of France.

Achille Mbembe (b. 1957) is a French Cameroonian philosopher and public intellectual, currently at the University of Witwatersrand in South Africa.

Albert Memmi (b. 1920) is a Tunisian author and cultural theorist, who writes both fiction and postcolonial criticism.

John Stuart Mill (1806–73) was an English philosopher and political economist, associated with the utilitarian school and liberal politics.

Huey P. Newton (1942–89) was an African American political activist and a founding member of the Black Panther Party.

Nghe Nguyen was a Vietnamese Marxist.

Antoine Porot (1876–1965) was a French psychiatrist who was notable for attempting to justify French colonial abuse in Africa.

Kate Reed is a lecturer in medical sociology at the University of Sheffield in the United Kingdom.

Edward Said (1935–2003) was a Palestinian American literary critic and public intellectual. His book *Orientalism* is among the seminal works of postcolonialism.

Bobby Sands (1954–81) was a member of the Provisional Irish Republican Army (Provisional IRA); he is notable for his long hunger strike in jail, eventually dying of starvation.

Jean-Paul Sartre (1905–80) was a French philosopher, literary critic, and public intellectual. Among his intellectual contributions, one of the most significant is the philosophy of existentialism, which holds that one's own existence and actions define what one "is" ("existence precedes essence").

Bobby Seale (b. 1936) is an African American political activist and member of the Black Panther Party.

Juan Ginés de Sepúlveda (c. 1489–c. 1573) was a Spanish philosopher. He was notable for claiming that indigenous Americans were "natural slaves."

Ali Shariati (1933–77) was an Iranian intellectual and major figure in the Iranian Revolution. He argued that the new government should be Islamic in character and presided over by a religious council.

Tracy Denean Sharpley-Whiting is a feminist thinker and professor of French at Vanderbilt University in the United States. She is notable for her focus on the intersection of race and gender.

Gayatri Spivak (b. 1942) is professor of comparative literature and society at Columbia University. Her work is notable for pointing out ways in which even well-meaning intellectuals can harm the colonial subject.

Gary Wilder is an associate professor of history at the City University of New York.

Robert C. Young (b. 1950) is a British postcolonial theorist. His book *White Mythologies* helped render "postcolonialism" a distinctive discipline.

WORKS CITED

WORKS CITED

Arendt, Hannah. *On Violence*. New York: Harcourt Brace, 1969.

"A Special Supplement: Reflections on Violence." *New York Review of Books*, February 27, 1969. Accessed October 4, 2015. http://www.nybooks.com/articles/archives/1969/feb/27/a-special-supplement-reflections-on-violence/.

Ashcroft, Bill, Gareth Griffiths, and Helen Tiffin. *The Empire Writes Back: Theory and Practice in Post-Colonial Literatures*. London: Routledge, 1989.

Beckett, Paul A. "Algeria vs. Fanon: The Theory of Revolutionary Decolonization, and the Algerian Experience." *Western Political Quarterly* 26, no. 1 (1973): 5–27.

Bentham, Jeremy. *Emancipate Your Colonies: Addressed to the National Convention of France*. London: Robert Heward, 1830.

Bercovitch, Sacvan, ed. *The Cambridge History of American Literature: Volume I 1590–1820*. Cambridge: Cambridge University Press, 1994.

Bernasconi, Robert. "Fanon's *The Wretched of the Earth* as the Fulfillment of Sartre's *Critique of Dialectical Reason*." *Sartre Studies International* 16, no. 2 (2010): 36–47.

Bhabha, Homi. "Remembering Fanon." *New Formations* 1 (1987): 118–24.

The Location of Culture. London: Routledge, 1994.

Burke III, Edmund. "Frantz Fanon's 'The Wretched of the Earth.'" *Daedalus* 105, no. 1 (1976): 127–35.

Césaire, Aimé. *Discourse on Colonialism*. Translated by Joan Pinkham. New York: Monthly Review Press, 2000.

Chamberlain, Muriel. *Longman Companion to European Decolonisation in the Twentieth Century*. Oxford: Routledge, 2013.

Cherki, Alice. *Frantz Fanon: A Portrait*. Translated by Nadia Benabid. Ithaca, NY: Cornell University Press, 2006.

Dabashi, Hamid. *Brown Skin, White Masks*. London: Pluto Press, 2011.

Du Bois, W. E. B. *The Souls of Black Folk: The Oxford W. E. B. Du Bois, Volume 3*. Edited by Henry Louis Gates, Jr. Oxford: Oxford University Press, 2007.

Egan, Daniel. "Frantz Fanon and the Construction of the Colonial Subject: Defining 'The Enemy' in the Iraq War." *Socialism and Democracy* 21, no. 3 (2007): 142–54.

Fanon, Frantz. *A Dying Colonialism*. Translated by Haakon Chevalier. New York: Grove Press, 1965.

———. *Toward The African Revolution*. Translated by Haakon Chevalier. New York: Grove Press, 1965.

———. *Black Skin, White Masks*. Translated by Charles Lam Markmann. London: Pluto Press, 1986.

———. *The Wretched of the Earth*. Translated by Constance Farrington. London: Penguin, 2001.

———. *The Wretched of the Earth*. Translated by Richard Philcox. New York: Grove Press, 2004.

———. *Black Skin, White Masks*. Translated by Charles Lam Markmann. London: Pluto Press, 2008.

Gates, Jr., Henry Louis. "Critical Fanonism." *Critical Inquiry* 17, no. 3 (1991): 457–70.

Gibson, Nigel. "Is Fanon Relevant? Toward an Alternative Foreword to 'The Damned of the Earth.'" *Human Architecture* 5, no. 3 (2007): 33–43.

Gikandi, Simon. "Poststructuralism and Postcolonial Discourse." In *The Cambridge Companion to Postcolonial Literary Studies*, edited by Neil Lazarus, 97–119. Cambridge: Cambridge University Press, 2004.

Gilroy, Paul. *The Black Atlantic: Modernity and Double Consciousness*. Cambridge, MA: Harvard University Press, 1993.

Hansen, Emmanuel. "Frantz Fanon: Portrait of a Revolutionary Intellectual." *Transition* 46 (1974): 25–36.

Huntington, Samuel. *The Clash of Civilizations and the Remaking of World Order*. London: Simon and Schuster, 2002.

Ismael, Jacqueline S., and Shereen T. Ismael. "The Arab Spring and the Uncivil State." *Arab Studies Quarterly* 35, no. 3 (2013): 229–40.

JanMohamed, Abdul R. "The Economy of Manichean Allegory: The Function of Racial Difference in Colonialist Literature." *Critical Inquiry* 12, no. 1 (1985): 59–87.

Jinadu, L. Adele. *Fanon: In Search of the African Revolution*. London: KPI, 1986.

Katrak, Ketu. "Decolonizing Culture: Toward a Theory for Postcolonial Women's Texts." *MFS Modern Fiction Studies* 35, no. 1 (1989): 157–79.

Keller, Richard C. "Clinician and Revolutionary: Frantz Fanon, Biography, and the History of Colonial Medicine." *Bulletin of the History of Medicine* 81, no. 4 (2007): 823–41.

Lazarus, Neil. "Disavowing Decolonization: Fanon, Nationalism, and the Problematic of Representation in Current Theories of Colonial Discourse." *Research in African Literatures* 24, no. 4 (1993): 69–98.

Lenin, Vladimir. *Imperialism: The Highest Stage of Capitalism*. Sydney: Resistance Books, 1999.

Lewis, Bernard. "The Roots of Muslim Rage." *The Atlantic* 266, no. 3 (1990): 47–60.

Macey, David. *Frantz Fanon: A Biography*. London: Verso, 2012.

Mannoni, Octave. *Prospero and Caliban: The Psychology of Colonization*. Translated by Pamela Powesland. Ann Arbor: University of Michigan Press, 1990.

Martin, Guy. "Fanon's Relevance to Contemporary African Political Thought." *Ufahamu: A Journal of African Studies* 4, no. 3 (1974): 11–34.

Mbembe, Achille. "Necropolitics." Translated by Libby Meintjes. *Public Culture* 15, no. 1 (2003): 11–40.

"Metamorphic Thought: The Works of Frantz Fanon." *African Studies* 71, no. 1 (2012): 19–28.

Memmi, Albert. *The Colonizer and the Colonized*. Boston, MA: Beacon Press, 1991.

Munif, Yasser. "Frantz Fanon and the Arab Uprisings: An Interview with Nigel Gibson." *Jadaliyya*, August 17, 2012. Accessed October 5, 2015. http://www.jadaliyya.com/pages/index/6927/frantz-fanon-and-the-arab-uprisings_an-interview-w.

Parry, Benita. "The Postcolonial: Conceptual Category or Chimera?" *Yearbook of English Studies* 27 (1997): 3–21.

Reed, Kate. *New Directions in Social Theory: Race, Gender, and the Canon*. London: Sage, 2006.

Robinson, Cedric. "The Appropriation of Frantz Fanon." *Race & Class* 35, no. 1 (1993): 79–91.

Said, Edward. *Orientalism*. New York: Random House, 1994.

Sartre, Jean-Paul. "Black Orpheus." *Massachusetts Review* 6, no. 1 (1964–5): 13–52.

Critique of Dialectical Reason Volume One. Translated by Alan Sheridan-Smith. London: Verso, 2004.

Seale, Bobby. *Seize the Time: The Story of the Black Panther Party and Huey P. Newton*. Baltimore, MD: Black Classic Press, 1991.

Sharpley-Whiting, T. Denean. *Frantz Fanon: Conflicts and Feminisms*. Lanham, MD: Rowman and Littlefield, 1998.

Spivak, Gayatri. "Can the Subaltern Speak?" In *Marxism and the Interpretation of Culture*, edited by Cary Nelson and Lawrence Grossberg, 271–313. Urbana: University of Illinois Press, 1988.

"Terror: A Speech after 9/11," *boundary 2* 31, no. 2 (2004): 81–111.

Sullivan, Eileen. "Liberalism and Imperialism: J. S. Mill's Defence of the British Empire." *Journal of the History of Ideas* 44, no. 4 (1983): 599–617.

United Nations. *Charter of the United Nations*, Article 73, October 24, 1945. Accessed October 2, 2015. www.un.org/en/documents/charter/chapter11.shtml.

Declaration on the Granting of Independence to Colonial Countries and Peoples, December 14, 1960. Accessed October 3, 2015. www.un.org/en/decolonization/declaration.shtml.

Wilder, Gary. *The French Imperial Nation State: Negritude and Colonial Humanism Between the Two World Wars*. Chicago: University of Chicago Press, 2005.

Young, Robert J. C. *Postcolonialism: An Historical Introduction*. Oxford: Blackwell, 2001.

THE MACAT LIBRARY
BY DISCIPLINE

AFRICANA STUDIES

Chinua Achebe's *An Image of Africa: Racism in Conrad's Heart of Darkness*
W. E. B. Du Bois's *The Souls of Black Folk*
Zora Neale Huston's *Characteristics of Negro Expression*
Martin Luther King Jr's *Why We Can't Wait*
Toni Morrison's *Playing in the Dark: Whiteness in the American Literary Imagination*

ANTHROPOLOGY

Arjun Appadurai's *Modernity at Large: Cultural Dimensions of Globalisation*
Philippe Ariès's *Centuries of Childhood*
Franz Boas's *Race, Language and Culture*
Kim Chan & Renée Mauborgne's *Blue Ocean Strategy*
Jared Diamond's *Guns, Germs & Steel: the Fate of Human Societies*
Jared Diamond's *Collapse: How Societies Choose to Fail or Survive*
E. E. Evans-Pritchard's *Witchcraft, Oracles and Magic Among the Azande*
James Ferguson's *The Anti-Politics Machine*
Clifford Geertz's *The Interpretation of Cultures*
David Graeber's *Debt: the First 5000 Years*
Karen Ho's *Liquidated: An Ethnography of Wall Street*
Geert Hofstede's *Culture's Consequences: Comparing Values, Behaviors, Institutes and Organizations across Nations*
Claude Lévi-Strauss's *Structural Anthropology*
Jay Macleod's *Ain't No Makin' It: Aspirations and Attainment in a Low-Income Neighborhood*
Saba Mahmood's *The Politics of Piety: The Islamic Revival and the Feminist Subject*
Marcel Mauss's *The Gift*

BUSINESS

Jean Lave & Etienne Wenger's *Situated Learning*
Theodore Levitt's *Marketing Myopia*
Burton G. Malkiel's *A Random Walk Down Wall Street*
Douglas McGregor's *The Human Side of Enterprise*
Michael Porter's *Competitive Strategy: Creating and Sustaining Superior Performance*
John Kotter's *Leading Change*
C. K. Prahalad & Gary Hamel's *The Core Competence of the Corporation*

CRIMINOLOGY

Michelle Alexander's *The New Jim Crow: Mass Incarceration in the Age of Colorblindness*
Michael R. Gottfredson & Travis Hirschi's *A General Theory of Crime*
Richard Herrnstein & Charles A. Murray's *The Bell Curve: Intelligence and Class Structure in American Life*
Elizabeth Loftus's *Eyewitness Testimony*
Jay Macleod's *Ain't No Makin' It: Aspirations and Attainment in a Low-Income Neighborhood*
Philip Zimbardo's *The Lucifer Effect*

ECONOMICS

Janet Abu-Lughod's *Before European Hegemony*
Ha-Joon Chang's *Kicking Away the Ladder*
David Brion Davis's *The Problem of Slavery in the Age of Revolution*
Milton Friedman's *The Role of Monetary Policy*
Milton Friedman's *Capitalism and Freedom*
David Graeber's *Debt: the First 5000 Years*
Friedrich Hayek's *The Road to Serfdom*
Karen Ho's *Liquidated: An Ethnography of Wall Street*

John Maynard Keynes's *The General Theory of Employment, Interest and Money*
Charles P. Kindleberger's *Manias, Panics and Crashes*
Robert Lucas's *Why Doesn't Capital Flow from Rich to Poor Countries?*
Burton G. Malkiel's *A Random Walk Down Wall Street*
Thomas Robert Malthus's *An Essay on the Principle of Population*
Karl Marx's *Capital*
Thomas Piketty's *Capital in the Twenty-First Century*
Amartya Sen's *Development as Freedom*
Adam Smith's *The Wealth of Nations*
Nassim Nicholas Taleb's *The Black Swan: The Impact of the Highly Improbable*
Amos Tversky's & Daniel Kahneman's *Judgment under Uncertainty: Heuristics and Biases*
Mahbub Ul Haq's *Reflections on Human Development*
Max Weber's *The Protestant Ethic and the Spirit of Capitalism*

FEMINISM AND GENDER STUDIES

Judith Butler's *Gender Trouble*
Simone De Beauvoir's *The Second Sex*
Michel Foucault's *History of Sexuality*
Betty Friedan's *The Feminine Mystique*
Saba Mahmood's *The Politics of Piety: The Islamic Revival and the Feminist Subject*
Joan Wallach Scott's *Gender and the Politics of History*
Mary Wollstonecraft's *A Vindication of the Rights of Women*
Virginia Woolf's *A Room of One's Own*

GEOGRAPHY

The Brundtland Report's *Our Common Future*
Rachel Carson's *Silent Spring*
Charles Darwin's *On the Origin of Species*
James Ferguson's *The Anti-Politics Machine*
Jane Jacobs's *The Death and Life of Great American Cities*
James Lovelock's *Gaia: A New Look at Life on Earth*
Amartya Sen's *Development as Freedom*
Mathis Wackernagel & William Rees's *Our Ecological Footprint*

HISTORY

Janet Abu-Lughod's *Before European Hegemony*
Benedict Anderson's *Imagined Communities*
Bernard Bailyn's *The Ideological Origins of the American Revolution*
Hanna Batatu's *The Old Social Classes And The Revolutionary Movements Of Iraq*
Christopher Browning's *Ordinary Men: Reserve Police Batallion 101 and the Final Solution in Poland*
Edmund Burke's *Reflections on the Revolution in France*
William Cronon's *Nature's Metropolis: Chicago And The Great West*
Alfred W. Crosby's *The Columbian Exchange*
Hamid Dabashi's *Iran: A People Interrupted*
David Brion Davis's *The Problem of Slavery in the Age of Revolution*
Nathalie Zemon Davis's *The Return of Martin Guerre*
Jared Diamond's *Guns, Germs & Steel: the Fate of Human Societies*
Frank Dikotter's *Mao's Great Famine*
John W Dower's *War Without Mercy: Race And Power In The Pacific War*
W. E. B. Du Bois's *The Souls of Black Folk*
Richard J. Evans's *In Defence of History*
Lucien Febvre's *The Problem of Unbelief in the 16th Century*
Sheila Fitzpatrick's *Everyday Stalinism*

Eric Foner's *Reconstruction: America's Unfinished Revolution, 1863-1877*
Michel Foucault's *Discipline and Punish*
Michel Foucault's *History of Sexuality*
Francis Fukuyama's *The End of History and the Last Man*
John Lewis Gaddis's *We Now Know: Rethinking Cold War History*
Ernest Gellner's *Nations and Nationalism*
Eugene Genovese's *Roll, Jordan, Roll: The World the Slaves Made*
Carlo Ginzburg's *The Night Battles*
Daniel Goldhagen's *Hitler's Willing Executioners*
Jack Goldstone's *Revolution and Rebellion in the Early Modern World*
Antonio Gramsci's *The Prison Notebooks*
Alexander Hamilton, John Jay & James Madison's *The Federalist Papers*
Christopher Hill's *The World Turned Upside Down*
Carole Hillenbrand's *The Crusades: Islamic Perspectives*
Thomas Hobbes's *Leviathan*
Eric Hobsbawm's *The Age Of Revolution*
John A. Hobson's *Imperialism: A Study*
Albert Hourani's *History of the Arab Peoples*
Samuel P. Huntington's *The Clash of Civilizations and the Remaking of World Order*
C. L. R. James's *The Black Jacobins*
Tony Judt's *Postwar: A History of Europe Since 1945*
Ernst Kantorowicz's *The King's Two Bodies: A Study in Medieval Political Theology*
Paul Kennedy's *The Rise and Fall of the Great Powers*
Ian Kershaw's *The "Hitler Myth": Image and Reality in the Third Reich*
John Maynard Keynes's *The General Theory of Employment, Interest and Money*
Charles P. Kindleberger's *Manias, Panics and Crashes*
Martin Luther King Jr's *Why We Can't Wait*
Henry Kissinger's *World Order: Reflections on the Character of Nations and the Course of History*
Thomas Kuhn's *The Structure of Scientific Revolutions*
Georges Lefebvre's *The Coming of the French Revolution*
John Locke's *Two Treatises of Government*
Niccolò Machiavelli's *The Prince*
Thomas Robert Malthus's *An Essay on the Principle of Population*
Mahmood Mamdani's *Citizen and Subject: Contemporary Africa And The Legacy Of Late Colonialism*
Karl Marx's *Capital*
Stanley Milgram's *Obedience to Authority*
John Stuart Mill's *On Liberty*
Thomas Paine's *Common Sense*
Thomas Paine's *Rights of Man*
Geoffrey Parker's *Global Crisis: War, Climate Change and Catastrophe in the Seventeenth Century*
Jonathan Riley-Smith's *The First Crusade and the Idea of Crusading*
Jean-Jacques Rousseau's *The Social Contract*
Joan Wallach Scott's *Gender and the Politics of History*
Theda Skocpol's *States and Social Revolutions*
Adam Smith's *The Wealth of Nations*
Timothy Snyder's *Bloodlands: Europe Between Hitler and Stalin*
Sun Tzu's *The Art of War*
Keith Thomas's *Religion and the Decline of Magic*
Thucydides's *The History of the Peloponnesian War*
Frederick Jackson Turner's *The Significance of the Frontier in American History*
Odd Arne Westad's *The Global Cold War: Third World Interventions And The Making Of Our Times*

LITERATURE

Chinua Achebe's *An Image of Africa: Racism in Conrad's Heart of Darkness*
Roland Barthes's *Mythologies*
Homi K. Bhabha's *The Location of Culture*
Judith Butler's *Gender Trouble*
Simone De Beauvoir's *The Second Sex*
Ferdinand De Saussure's *Course in General Linguistics*
T. S. Eliot's *The Sacred Wood: Essays on Poetry and Criticism*
Zora Neale Huston's *Characteristics of Negro Expression*
Toni Morrison's *Playing in the Dark: Whiteness in the American Literary Imagination*
Edward Said's *Orientalism*
Gayatri Chakravorty Spivak's *Can the Subaltern Speak?*
Mary Wollstonecraft's *A Vindication of the Rights of Women*
Virginia Woolf's *A Room of One's Own*

PHILOSOPHY

Elizabeth Anscombe's *Modern Moral Philosophy*
Hannah Arendt's *The Human Condition*
Aristotle's *Metaphysics*
Aristotle's *Nicomachean Ethics*
Edmund Gettier's *Is Justified True Belief Knowledge?*
Georg Wilhelm Friedrich Hegel's *Phenomenology of Spirit*
David Hume's *Dialogues Concerning Natural Religion*
David Hume's *The Enquiry for Human Understanding*
Immanuel Kant's *Religion within the Boundaries of Mere Reason*
Immanuel Kant's *Critique of Pure Reason*
Søren Kierkegaard's *The Sickness Unto Death*
Søren Kierkegaard's *Fear and Trembling*
C. S. Lewis's *The Abolition of Man*
Alasdair MacIntyre's *After Virtue*
Marcus Aurelius's *Meditations*
Friedrich Nietzsche's *On the Genealogy of Morality*
Friedrich Nietzsche's *Beyond Good and Evil*
Plato's *Republic*
Plato's *Symposium*
Jean-Jacques Rousseau's *The Social Contract*
Gilbert Ryle's *The Concept of Mind*
Baruch Spinoza's *Ethics*
Sun Tzu's *The Art of War*
Ludwig Wittgenstein's *Philosophical Investigations*

POLITICS

Benedict Anderson's *Imagined Communities*
Aristotle's *Politics*
Bernard Bailyn's *The Ideological Origins of the American Revolution*
Edmund Burke's *Reflections on the Revolution in France*
John C. Calhoun's *A Disquisition on Government*
Ha-Joon Chang's *Kicking Away the Ladder*
Hamid Dabashi's *Iran: A People Interrupted*
Hamid Dabashi's *Theology of Discontent: The Ideological Foundation of the Islamic Revolution in Iran*
Robert Dahl's *Democracy and its Critics*
Robert Dahl's *Who Governs?*
David Brion Davis's *The Problem of Slavery in the Age of Revolution*

Alexis De Tocqueville's *Democracy in America*
James Ferguson's *The Anti-Politics Machine*
Frank Dikotter's *Mao's Great Famine*
Sheila Fitzpatrick's *Everyday Stalinism*
Eric Foner's *Reconstruction: America's Unfinished Revolution, 1863-1877*
Milton Friedman's *Capitalism and Freedom*
Francis Fukuyama's *The End of History and the Last Man*
John Lewis Gaddis's *We Now Know: Rethinking Cold War History*
Ernest Gellner's *Nations and Nationalism*
David Graeber's *Debt: the First 5000 Years*
Antonio Gramsci's *The Prison Notebooks*
Alexander Hamilton, John Jay & James Madison's *The Federalist Papers*
Friedrich Hayek's *The Road to Serfdom*
Christopher Hill's *The World Turned Upside Down*
Thomas Hobbes's *Leviathan*
John A. Hobson's *Imperialism: A Study*
Samuel P. Huntington's *The Clash of Civilizations and the Remaking of World Order*
Tony Judt's *Postwar: A History of Europe Since 1945*
David C. Kang's *China Rising: Peace, Power and Order in East Asia*
Paul Kennedy's *The Rise and Fall of Great Powers*
Robert Keohane's *After Hegemony*
Martin Luther King Jr.'s *Why We Can't Wait*
Henry Kissinger's *World Order: Reflections on the Character of Nations and the Course of History*
John Locke's *Two Treatises of Government*
Niccolò Machiavelli's *The Prince*
Thomas Robert Malthus's *An Essay on the Principle of Population*
Mahmood Mamdani's *Citizen and Subject: Contemporary Africa And The Legacy Of Late Colonialism*
Karl Marx's *Capital*
John Stuart Mill's *On Liberty*
John Stuart Mill's *Utilitarianism*
Hans Morgenthau's *Politics Among Nations*
Thomas Paine's *Common Sense*
Thomas Paine's *Rights of Man*
Thomas Piketty's *Capital in the Twenty-First Century*
Robert D. Putman's *Bowling Alone*
John Rawls's *Theory of Justice*
Jean-Jacques Rousseau's *The Social Contract*
Theda Skocpol's *States and Social Revolutions*
Adam Smith's *The Wealth of Nations*
Sun Tzu's *The Art of War*
Henry David Thoreau's *Civil Disobedience*
Thucydides's *The History of the Peloponnesian War*
Kenneth Waltz's *Theory of International Politics*
Max Weber's *Politics as a Vocation*
Odd Arne Westad's *The Global Cold War: Third World Interventions And The Making Of Our Times*

POSTCOLONIAL STUDIES

Roland Barthes's *Mythologies*
Frantz Fanon's *Black Skin, White Masks*
Homi K. Bhabha's *The Location of Culture*
Gustavo Gutiérrez's *A Theology of Liberation*
Edward Said's *Orientalism*
Gayatri Chakravorty Spivak's *Can the Subaltern Speak?*

PSYCHOLOGY

Gordon Allport's *The Nature of Prejudice*
Alan Baddeley & Graham Hitch's *Aggression: A Social Learning Analysis*
Albert Bandura's *Aggression: A Social Learning Analysis*
Leon Festinger's *A Theory of Cognitive Dissonance*
Sigmund Freud's *The Interpretation of Dreams*
Betty Friedan's *The Feminine Mystique*
Michael R. Gottfredson & Travis Hirschi's *A General Theory of Crime*
Eric Hoffer's *The True Believer: Thoughts on the Nature of Mass Movements*
William James's *Principles of Psychology*
Elizabeth Loftus's *Eyewitness Testimony*
A. H. Maslow's *A Theory of Human Motivation*
Stanley Milgram's *Obedience to Authority*
Steven Pinker's *The Better Angels of Our Nature*
Oliver Sacks's *The Man Who Mistook His Wife For a Hat*
Richard Thaler & Cass Sunstein's *Nudge: Improving Decisions About Health, Wealth and Happiness*
Amos Tversky's *Judgment under Uncertainty: Heuristics and Biases*
Philip Zimbardo's *The Lucifer Effect*

SCIENCE

Rachel Carson's *Silent Spring*
William Cronon's *Nature's Metropolis: Chicago And The Great West*
Alfred W. Crosby's *The Columbian Exchange*
Charles Darwin's *On the Origin of Species*
Richard Dawkin's *The Selfish Gene*
Thomas Kuhn's *The Structure of Scientific Revolutions*
Geoffrey Parker's *Global Crisis: War, Climate Change and Catastrophe in the Seventeenth Century*
Mathis Wackernagel & William Rees's *Our Ecological Footprint*

SOCIOLOGY

Michelle Alexander's *The New Jim Crow: Mass Incarceration in the Age of Colorblindness*
Gordon Allport's *The Nature of Prejudice*
Albert Bandura's *Aggression: A Social Learning Analysis*
Hanna Batatu's *The Old Social Classes And The Revolutionary Movements Of Iraq*
Ha-Joon Chang's *Kicking Away the Ladder*
W. E. B. Du Bois's *The Souls of Black Folk*
Émile Durkheim's *On Suicide*
Frantz Fanon's *Black Skin, White Masks*
Frantz Fanon's *The Wretched of the Earth*
Eric Foner's *Reconstruction: America's Unfinished Revolution, 1863-1877*
Eugene Genovese's *Roll, Jordan, Roll: The World the Slaves Made*
Jack Goldstone's *Revolution and Rebellion in the Early Modern World*
Antonio Gramsci's *The Prison Notebooks*
Richard Herrnstein & Charles A Murray's *The Bell Curve: Intelligence and Class Structure in American Life*
Eric Hoffer's *The True Believer: Thoughts on the Nature of Mass Movements*
Jane Jacobs's *The Death and Life of Great American Cities*
Robert Lucas's *Why Doesn't Capital Flow from Rich to Poor Countries?*
Jay Macleod's *Ain't No Makin' It: Aspirations and Attainment in a Low Income Neighborhood*
Elaine May's *Homeward Bound: American Families in the Cold War Era*
Douglas McGregor's *The Human Side of Enterprise*
C. Wright Mills's *The Sociological Imagination*

Thomas Piketty's *Capital in the Twenty-First Century*
Robert D. Putman's *Bowling Alone*
David Riesman's *The Lonely Crowd: A Study of the Changing American Character*
Edward Said's *Orientalism*
Joan Wallach Scott's *Gender and the Politics of History*
Theda Skocpol's *States and Social Revolutions*
Max Weber's *The Protestant Ethic and the Spirit of Capitalism*

THEOLOGY

Augustine's *Confessions*
Benedict's *Rule of St Benedict*
Gustavo Gutiérrez's *A Theology of Liberation*
Carole Hillenbrand's *The Crusades: Islamic Perspectives*
David Hume's *Dialogues Concerning Natural Religion*
Immanuel Kant's *Religion within the Boundaries of Mere Reason*
Ernst Kantorowicz's *The King's Two Bodies: A Study in Medieval Political Theology*
Søren Kierkegaard's *The Sickness Unto Death*
C. S. Lewis's *The Abolition of Man*
Saba Mahmood's *The Politics of Piety: The Islamic Revival and the Feminist Subject*
Baruch Spinoza's *Ethics*
Keith Thomas's *Religion and the Decline of Magic*

COMING SOON

Chris Argyris's *The Individual and the Organisation*
Seyla Benhabib's *The Rights of Others*
Walter Benjamin's *The Work Of Art in the Age of Mechanical Reproduction*
John Berger's *Ways of Seeing*
Pierre Bourdieu's *Outline of a Theory of Practice*
Mary Douglas's *Purity and Danger*
Roland Dworkin's *Taking Rights Seriously*
James G. March's *Exploration and Exploitation in Organisational Learning*
Ikujiro Nonaka's *A Dynamic Theory of Organizational Knowledge Creation*
Griselda Pollock's *Vision and Difference*
Amartya Sen's *Inequality Re-Examined*
Susan Sontag's *On Photography*
Yasser Tabbaa's *The Transformation of Islamic Art*
Ludwig von Mises's *Theory of Money and Credit*

9 781912 128532

Poems from the Wilderness

Jack Mayer

Proverse Hong Kong

2020

The front cover image by Justin P. Goodhart was taken at the West Mountain Shelter along the Appalachian Trail in New York State.

Wilderness inspired poems composed on the trail by an American doctor/poet, sharing his love of the backcountry, trail-walking, camping, and the "wilderness effect," a unique sensation of aliveness and deep connection. Mayer's poetry explores our human experience of the natural world, our intimate and mysterious connections to flora and fauna. It proclaims the opportunity that walking mindfully in the wilderness offers to experience the divine. The uniqueness and intensity of these musings lead his poems to attempt reconciliation of our lived experience with physics, spirit, and music, the latter manifested in his experience of singing to the dying; the wisdom of nature rendered in music and consolation. A few poems are inspired by Mayer's medical practice. Some spring from his ordinary life and reflections on his childhood and family, which have followed him into the woods.

Jack Mayer is a Vermont writer and pediatrician. He was an anti-Vietnam war activist in the '60s and was arrested at a demonstration in Chicago in 1969. His legal case, argued before the U.S. Supreme Court (Mayer vs. City of Chicago, 1971), established the right of indigents to have court costs paid by the state. (By the time he was in medical school he had college and medical school debts. His only valuable possessions were his microscope and textbooks. In a *New York Times* article about his trial, the Chicago judge was quoted as expressing his surprise that in America a medical student could be judged an indigent.)

In 1976 Dr Mayer established the first pediatric practice in Vermont's Eastern Franklin County on the Canadian border, where he began writing about his practice and hiking Vermont's Long Trail. In the '80s Mayer was an anti-nuclear activist and New England delegate to **Physicians for Social Responsibility**.

Dr Mayer was a National Cancer Institute Fellow at **Columbia University,** researching the molecular biology of cancer (1987-1991). He established **Rainbow Pediatrics** in Middlebury, Vermont, in 1991 and continues to practice pediatrics there. He is an Instructor in Pediatrics at the **University of Vermont School of Medicine** and a pre-med mentor at **Middlebury College**. He was a participant at the **Bread Loaf Writers' Conference** in 2003 and 2005 (fiction) and 2008 (poetry). His first non-fiction book is *Life In A Jar: The Irena Sendler Project*. His new book, *Before The Court Of Heaven*, is historical fiction.

Poems from the Wilderness

Jack Mayer
"Mountain Poet"

Winner of the Proverse Prize 2019

Proverse Hong Kong

Poems from the Wilderness
By Jack Mayer ("Mountain Poet").
First edition published in paperback in Hong Kong
by Proverse Hong Kong, under sole and exclusive licence,
April/November 2020.
ISBN 13: 978-988-8491-87-2

Enquiries to Proverse Hong Kong
P.O. Box 259, Tung Chung Post Office,
Lantau, NT, Hong Kong SAR, China.
Email: proverse@netvigator.com;
Web: www.proversepublishing.com

Cover photo by and courtesy of Justin P. Goodhart.
Author photo by Chip Mayer.
Cover design by Artist Hong Kong.

British Library Cataloguing in Publication Data
A catalogue record for the first paperback edition
is available from the British Library

Prior Publication Acknowledgements

Mayer, J.L. 'Grand Union,' (poem), *Friends Journal, Quaker Thought and Life Today*. 46 (2) February 2000
Mayer, J.L. 'Umbilical Wormhole,' (poem), website of William Carter, Photographer, for his book Illuminations, e-publication, www.editionsone.com, 2003.
Mayer, J.L. 'Maps,' (poem), *Long Trail News*, 73(1) Spring 2013.
Mayer, J.L. 'I am a God to the Birds' (poem) 1st Prize – Proverse International Poetry contest 2017. *Mingled Voices 2: The International Proverse Poetry Prize Anthology 2017*, Volume 2, March 1, 2018
Mayer, J.L. 'Stubbornly Persistent Illusion' (poem), *Addison Independent*, Poet's Corner, Jan. 11, 2018
Mayer, J.L. 'Psalm 23/Hospice Volunteer' (poem) 3rd Prize – Proverse International Poetry contest 2018. *Mingled Voices 3: The International Proverse Poetry Prize Anthology 2018*, Volume 3, March 2019
Mayer, J.L. 'God Particle' (poem) *Mingled Voices 3: The International Proverse Poetry Prize Anthology 2018*, Volume 3, March 2019
Mayer, J.L. 'Blood' (poem) *Mingled Voices 3: The International Proverse Poetry Prize Anthology 2018,* Volume 3, March 2019

Expression of Gratitude

I am deeply appreciative of Vermont poet Susan Jefts for her incisive and thoughtful editing. She helped me see the forest and the trees. I am also grateful to Gillian Bickley, co-founder and co-publisher of Proverse and co-founder of the Proverse Prizes, for her thoughtful and sensitive editorial contributions.

I am indebted to the Green Mountain Club (GMC) and the Appalachian Mountain Club (AMC) for being stewards and champions of Vermont's Long Trail, the Appalachian Trail and side trails, Vermont's splendor, her wilderness.

I salute the memory of Joseph Battell (1839 - 1915) from my hometown of Middlebury, Vermont. He was a publisher, conservationist, and philanthropist credited with preserving Vermont forest land including the Bread Loaf Wilderness and Camel's Hump State Park where I frequently hike. The Joseph Battell Wilderness in the Green Mountain National Forest bears his name.

Author's Introduction

I have been hiking Vermont's Long Trail and parts of the Appalachian Trail and White Mountains for forty years. On solo hikes and while backcountry skiing and snowshoeing, I compose a poem in my pocket notebook and copy it into a trail shelter logbook. Each entry is signed by the hiker's trail name – a name and identity adopted exclusively for walking in the wilderness. My own trail name is "Mountain Poet."

Off the trail, I am a primary care pediatrician in Vermont. Two of these poems are "doctor poems" composed on the trail in response to powerful and poignant interactions with my patients. ('Ellie's Second Baby' and 'Blood.') I began practicing medicine in a very rural area of northern Vermont, on the Canadian border in a town with the lowest income in the state of Vermont. Mine was the first pediatric practice in Eastern Franklin County and the need was great. I began writing poems about my patients as a way of understanding and empathizing with the challenges of their lives. 'Blood' is inspired by a house call during a snowstorm to an indigent family living in a trailer. 'Ellie's Second Baby' is my processing of an emergency Caesarean section and a critically ill baby.

Since semi-retiring from medicine, I have been a Hospice volunteer and singer in a Hospice singing group "Wellspring." We sing at the bedside for those nearing the end of life (another kind of wilderness) and their families. 'Psalm 23/Hospice Volunteer' and 'Singing Over' are inspired by my experiences with song and the end of life. They are also my tribute to the Hospice volunteers who minister to the dying with unconditional presence and love, with their generosity of time and spirit, holiness and grace made plain.

In the solitude of nature I have contemplated the cosmological wilderness. The intersection of metaphysics, physics, and spirit, another source of inspiration and composition.

Jack Mayer

For my son Alex
my fellow wilderness traveller

POEMS FROM THE WILDERNESS

PHYSICS

SPIRIT

MUSIC

FOREST

A Boy Is Missing

A boy is missing. I'm on his trail.

There is no alarm clock to wake me,
to propel me by internal combustion
over asphalt, sidewalks, deadlines,
into my extinct future.
Only a faint trail, white blazes
suggesting North, or South,
or sanctuary, the next water source,
last year's leaf mulch.

The boy I'm tracking down,
the boy whose trail I follow,
has been missing for so long
that I scarcely remember
his favorite flannel shirt,
his buck teeth and Brylcreem-stiff hair.
Mile by mile I draw closer
glimpse him through autumn foliage.
My hands and face are unwashed,
I carry soil into my tent
with neither worry nor culpability
and sleep the phantasmagorical sleep
of one newly born,
or one who has passed over.
Don't call me, there is no phone.
Don't send me to bed, there is no bed.
Don't fill my plate with boiled Brussels sprouts
or illusions I must swallow if I want dessert.

I won't ever find that missing boy,
but searching unbundles my soul.

Long Trail – Clarendon Shelter – 2010

Autumn / M.C. Escher

Spectral foliage floats
on azure sky's swift breeze.
M.C. Escher mosaics of leaves under foot.
Mezzo-throated thrush
sings only to me
(maybe it's true).
Countless springs and summers
I have walked these mountains.
Now it is my autumn
and these vistas are memoir.
Kaleidoscopic where once was only green,
patterns evolving, recurring
yet unique, like fractal bits
that contain a universe.
Nothing stays as it seems –
visual tricks, transitions,
painful and amusing,
as if one of our Gods
perceives us as billions of
Escher's September leaves
morphing into birds,
flying off the woodcut's edge.

Long Trail – Clarendon Shelter – PoemTown, Randolph, VT.
April 2015

ANOMALY: That which cannot be named
(with apologies to J.K. Rowling's, *Harry Potter* series)

Two millennia ago, Claudius Ptolemy, the Roman astronomer,
wrote his thirteen book treatise ***Almagest*** that explained
everything –
the motion of sun, moon, and planets,
every anomaly recalculated into nesting spheres of complexity,
of predictability, and coming out exactly right.
Except for his basic premise, from which all else flowed,
"The Earth is the center of the Universe."

Today, hiking up Mount Abe's flank,
in autumn's sacrificial red, yellow, orange, and brown,
I sense the quantum unraveling of particles and Quarks
and the stories they tell.
Serenity I know, is much more
than neurochemical serotonin, dopamine.
Two millennia from now what will they think
of our nesting spheres of complexity?

Two birds bicker ceaselessly in a beech tree,
bundles of chemicals, not unlike me.
I am their infrequent visitor, an anomaly in their universe,
not Ptolemy – not quantum – not dopamine.
Other,
      other.

The Long Trail – Battell Shelter – Mount Abraham
October 2013

Boundaries

I. Otter Creek

Rusted rail bridge reflection
shimmers like Monet's Water Lilies,
a delicate mass on Otter Creek.
Our red Old Town canoe
hovers on the boundary of two worlds,
paddles dripping and thrusting like lightning,
from one world to another.
We seem to float high in the water trees.

At the bow the Wild Woman,
burnt sienna hair aroused by the wind
at the fringe of her white baseball cap.
A northwest wind pushes us back upstream, hard.
"Forward, Relax. Forward, Relax,"
leaning forward, pulling back,
hypnotic propulsion with calm ferocity.
Our Old Towne canoe slices the waves
as surely as a first kiss cleaves the heart.

Leicester Junction, 3-mile Bridge, Middlebury, Weybridge,
Vergennes

Boundaries

II. Mount Abe

Scrape of slate on rock
echoing through leafless trees,
A blue jay screeching
in the rain expectant air.
Chipmunk crackles over crisp leaves.
The last moths of summer
try to keep aloft on geriatric wings
just inches over the mulch.
First snow dots the ground
from Halloween's storm.
Mount Abe's peak pierces the sky,
an island in the atmospheric sea.
The tide is high, the surf wild.

We live in the membrane between
the sea above and the Otter Creek below-
sweet space of illusion and consequence,
moth and snow.

Long Trail – Battell Shelter – 4 November 1994

Confusion

From Mount Abe's Stonehenge summit,
a round cairn from which
the Champlain Valley,
from Adirondacks to Green Mountains,
is a Chinese watercolour of mist on mountains.
One bleeds into the other.
I confuse the mist for the mountain,
the brook for the breeze –
God's breath for my own.

Long Trail – Battell Shelter –Mount Abraham – 27 June 2008

Incarnation

Invisible wind sings the leaves.
An acorn drops onto a leaf-strewn cemetery.
Young trees abound round old survivors,
some as old as me, some older.
The stone wall (how did it get here?)
three centuries old, still tells stories
I cannot understand.

Tonight I'm at The Secret Shelter –
"Swansong" – the last and best.
A perfect Long Trail evening
with fire and book.

I wake to rain on my tent
and hike through the drenched forest
carrying only my pack and my trail name.
Time slows to each step's rhythm,
glacial rock walls,
tree family generations.
A thrush high in a white pine
sings me back to a time I understand.
Soon enough, I'll be with the rocks and the trees.
I'll have a new trail name –
no longer "Mountain Poet."
Maybe "Sprout" or "Beetle" or
"Granite Mountain".

Long Trail – Swansong Shelter – The "Secret" Shelter
21 August 2010

Desire

When I was twelve
I mailed a comic book coupon,
hoping against hope
that I would be the kid
to win an electric Ford Thunderbird.
So badly I wanted it,
that as I stared
through the window of the M-100,
the Broadway bus from the Bronx to Washington Heights,
I imagined driving my shiny T-bird to Hebrew School.
I would park in front of Temple Beth-El
and stride into Mr. Gleason's classroom.
"Homework? I have three tests in 'real school.'
And besides that, I wouldn't have done it anyway."
My electric T-bird would carry me home
through the dark chill of November,
and I'd never wait for the M-100 again.

Today, desire dwells atop Mount Abe.
My heart anticipates, imagines the summit.
I sweat and scramble up steep boulders.
A mosquito pricks my arm,
as if my blood-meal could fill
the hole in its tiny heart.
Momentarily my cheek brushes what lies beyond,
out of reach, past imagination.

Deadly sins and lively pleasures –
so many wormholes to desire,
the final common pathway of
epiphany, sensuality and greed.
I am an addict to the poetry of desire,
the cruel disequilibrium
of meter and free verse.
And yes, I still want that T-bird.

Long Trail – Mount Abraham – Battell Shelter – 9 July 2001

The Library

On the dangerous side of Broadway,
hoods with slicked back hair
hung out at the pizza parlor.
Gangs prowled Washington Heights,
the pinched tip of Manhattan island.
There were zip-guns and switchblades across Broadway.
Not even President Ike,
the Liberator of Europe,
could change those matters of fact.

Then there was the library,
which smelled the way I imagined church scent.
Heavy wooden sanctuary doors shut out
the street sounds from Saint Nicholas Avenue,
leaving solemn silence,
reverence that made every child whisper,
safety that made them return.
Upstairs, in the adult reading room,
only shuffling and shifting, sniffing and sometimes snoring.
My mother protected us as we crossed Broadway,
back to our side again,
bringing our books back to Granny's apartment.
Her gnarled hands covered our heads
each time we left and again when we returned.
She mumbled the Priestly Blessing.
She seemed relieved we were safe,
and maybe she said so,
but only in German, or Hebrew,
never speaking other words
after *Kristallnacht*,
as if the shattered shards of her world,
wounds she still carried,
had crystallized.

My wife drops me off at the Brandon Gap trailhead.
Road noise fades.
I hear only my footfalls
and the crinkle of dead leaves.
The National Forest's heavy wooden doors
close behind me.
I am in the adult reading room – Sunrise Shelter –
three walls and a roof.
The rain ended a few hours ago.
Misty clouds lift

from the Great Cliffs of Mount Horrid
(what tales lay therein?).
My shelter mates,
"Rusted Root", and "Mops and Pops"
stare out from the shelter edge.
We are reading the world,
from the numinous reverence of The Library.

Long Trail – Sunrise Shelter – 4 August 2001

Kristallnacht: The "Night of Broken Glass":
a Nazi pogrom against Jews carried out by SA paramilitary forces and
civilians throughout Nazi Germany on 9–10 November 1938.

Rusted Root: trail name of a hiker at the shelter.

Mops and Pops: husband and wife. These were their trail names.

Adagio

Dawn spider webs brush my eyes
and I know I am the first
on this trail today.
Too early for the mosquito;
last night's revelry keeps him abed.
Fern-field choruses sing Hallelujah!
Leaves agitate with excess.
Summer light dapples
and the wet scent of contentment hovers.
Sawed logs, some rotting,
covered with moss,
bridge the boggy places
for we who yearn
for the adagio of wilderness.

I watch a sparrow
fitfully flit higher into a birch tree,
approaching his beloved
branch by branch.
Just inches apart,
two heads twitching,
fearful, scanning.
Suddenly, she flies away.
All that longing consumed
in an instant.

I climb no peaks today,
seek neither spectacular
nor definitive view,
only to share the woods
with a sad brown sparrow
scraping dead leaves
on this forest floor,
seeking grace.

Boyce Shelter – Long Trail – Skyline Lodge – 14 July 1993

Camperized

I'm waiting for my camp-coffee water to boil,
fueled by a gas-fired Pocket Rocket cook stove.
I spread SKIPPY smooth peanut butter
on a slice of Dave's Organic 12-Grain Bread.
By this age, I've accommodated the irony.

When my son went to a wilderness camp
he returned home "camperized."
Fingernail dirt lines, grime encrusted socks,
clothing stiff from sweat,
an over-used high school gym locker scent.

The last half-century has been eventful.
Right up there with Mars losing its atmosphere,
and the dinosaur extinction after an unfortunate collision.
It's a well-worn problem of us *Homo sapiens*,
the blessing and curse of our cleverness.
e.g. poetry, the computer
e.g. WWI, WWII, Korea, etc., etc.

Only one day in the wilderness
and I am thoroughly camperized,
like a boy in the backcountry
lured by the forest's pheromones.
But still, I contemplate how
the world is going crazy.
These woods offer the only true solace.
I treasure and cling
to that mote of Aquarian dust we all carry.
I am camperized,
a line of honest dirt in my heart,
the sole sound the forest.

Long Trail – Clarendon Shelter – 30 June 2018

Five Days on the Trail

I. Woodpecker

Downy Woodpecker, a small guy,
pecks at big wood.
A storm is brewing
and I'm still half a mile from Minerva Hinchey.

At the shelter, thunder
darkens the woods,
premonitory air hushed and still.
I feel something I can neither describe nor explain.
I have become "of the woods" –
just another creature of need and desire.

I trust the woodpecker found shelter
and after the storm passes
he will resume his meaningful tap, tap, tapping,
seeking food, a nest, a mate –
ultimately no different than my search
for sustenance, rest, continuity –
grace by any other name.

In the morning
a freshening wind blows
the rain to the east.
Soon as I finish my camp coffee
I'll pick up my trekking poles
and rejoin the trail –
tap, tap, tapping for essence,
for grace.

Minerva Hinchey Shelter

II. Tricks

"If the tricks of the night are explained, how can you appreciate the dark?" (*The Night Circus*, by Erin Morgenstern)

The tricks of mist,
a cloud obscuring and revealing,
swirling through trees,
the mystery of twilight,
the gourmet delight of peanut butter on Jewish Rye,
of Teriyaki Beef and Tex-Mex Mix . . .
and trail magic –
a plastic bag hanging on a tree
with candy and one bag of cashews – glazed
with pomegranate and vanilla.

Is the mist in the trees,
the whisper of wilderness,
God's sleight of hand?
Is twilight a magical disappearance,
and suddenly here is the Milky Way?
Why do we call it "trail magic"
instead of a gift?

Tomorrow I will visit the Cairn Garden
at White Rocks Overlook,
a museum of rock cairns,
built by hikers, by pilgrims,
and pay homage to the sacred and secular
magicians who play all these tricks.

Greenwell Shelter

III. Truckin'

Each mile is longer,
soon I'll be a-shufflin'.
Long as I can,
I'll keep on a-truckin'

Minerva Hinchey Shelter

IV. Communion

I am homesick for these woods,
anticipating their loss in frailty and death.
How humbling to carry everything
on my back,
for no human voice
to scatter the sanctity.

Today I am on no quest,
seeking only communion
in this temple.

Clarendon Shelter

The Long Trail – Clarendon Gorge – 12-16 September 2013

After life

My backcountry skis break trail
in the meadow below Robert Frost's cabin,
like a pen inscribing
a thought about eternity.
Who could know
what transpires after
the last breath,
the last electric tick?
Perhaps our next existence
is a memory,
a spark we share
but cannot perceive,
except in the approximation
of words and stories
we tell ourselves so we can sleep.

My wife offers Reiki meditation
at the Animal Shelter.
Dogs stop barking,
cats, once feral, curl in her lap
and purr energy
no one can explain.
Perhaps our perceptions
are pet-toys deployed
to occupy our monkey-minds,
(feral until not so long ago),
while everything else spins.

We live enshrouded,
barking at one another,
baying at the moon,
purring when we love,

waking at our passing
into the lap of grace.

Robert Frost cabin – Bread Loaf wilderness – 28 February 2018

Mist On Mount Abe

I climb up Battell Trail,
a spur off the Long Trail,
into Mount Abe's mist,
pastel painted for Fall.
Autumn insects awaken,
hung-over with summer's excess.
South wind stirs dying foliage,
not yet for the last time,
till they fall. Yellow leaves
my diamond-studded trail.

As "Mountain Poet",
I thank the earth for this
astounding writing desk,
this palette of water colours,
mist today, hard sun tomorrow.
The dying of the green.
Some of the 10,000 things
are lost, some gained.
One day I'll be here
as ashes, aching to be released.
Don't trap me in an urn,
rather pour my ashes into this earth,
return my atoms to the cosmos.
Spread some of me atop Mount Abe
for one last walk in the woods
from which I will not return.

Battell Shelter – on Mount Abraham – Long Trail
9 October 2018

Chiaroscuro

The atmospheric ocean is deep and still today,
torpid with Amazon humidity.
No breeze; suspended breath,
downy woodpecker tapping far away,
Doppler drone of flies about my head.

Chiaroscuro.
Chiaroscuro.
Just saying the word
my tongue feels its meaning –
play of light and dark,
green on green
in these woods.
Chiaroscuro.

My boot leather creaks
each footfall. Chiaroscuro –
play of sound and silence
in muted atmosphere.

At this Vermont trail head
Brush Brook sluices
and curves over
a finely polished boulder,
splashing up finally,
and falling, spent,
into the arms of a deep pool.

Long Trail – Montclair Glen Shelter – Camel's Hump – Forest City Trail – 30 June 1995

Contentment – A Quality

with acknowledgements to, *The Book of Qualities*, by Ruth
Gendler

Contentment lives alone, nestled
in the grandfather tree's roots in the Middlebury Gap.
Because I search for her, she flies away,
like the sparrow. Yet, I know she is near
in the peripheral vision of my desire.

Recently, I learned that Contentment is common born,
like moss. She is the first child
of Wind in the Leaves and Pine Forest Scent.
Sadly, Fortune is her grandmother –
stern and unfathomable, capricious to a fault.
She is not particularly fertile.

Do you wish to capture Contentment?
Keep her with you always?
You cannot, you must not,
for her elusiveness, her veil of "elusion,"
the essence of her allure,
is the heart of her charm.

Long Trail – Boyce Shelter – 14 July 1993

Gratitude

Thank you, Wilderness, my old, old friend
who, upon reunion after my year-long absence,
asks for nothing and gives everything.

When we first met, I knew you like a brother.
I was 8, you were 3.8 billion.
It was my first hike, with Uncle Eric
and his dachshund Bijou, in the Catskill Mountains.
In my early twenties, besotted with you,
zealously adolescent, I nearly froze to death
snow camping in the High Sierra near Donner Pass.

We have grown closer and older, you and I.
You have held me as I slept in my mummy sack.
My hiking sticks, once ornamental are now essential.
The sheer tonnage I have hauled to be near you
has lightened with miracle fibers.
The trail has become my enduring house of worship,
stained glass foliage praising forest saints.
I am penitent about the privies we humans have built
along our pilgrimage route,
clumsy, crude confessionals
for a communion of sorts.

Someday soon, we'll share a park bench,
you and I, on a sunny autumn day.
Tears will blur, because soon I will leave you,
and I will say, "Thank you," again.

Long Trail – Clarendon Shelter – 21 August 2017

TRAIL

Maps

My USGS topographical map,
Mansfield Quadrant, 1:25,000
reassures me through this
vast, rough wilderness.
Is it better to have a map?
To anticipate the steepness,
the danger? or
to just let each foot guide me?

Better not to know
that my son would roll the car,
that he would almost drown,
that his heart would be broken,
that my heart would be broken,
that tragedy stalks us.
Not to have known what I know today
was the wellspring of courage.

I learned all the maps.
Galileo, Columbus, Einstein,
all the imperfect imaginings
of creation.
Death was a complex biochemical cascade,
committed to memory in medical school.

Nevertheless, my topo map is reassuring.
The Nose of Mount Mansfield sticks up
behind Madonna Mountain's shoulder,
exactly where it should be.

Long Trail – Whiteface Shelter – July 2008

In Memoriam – SVEA Camp Stove

It rained hard yesterday at Middlebury Gap.
Deep footprints in the mud
will soon enough disappear.
The ridge line is enchanted with morning mist,
pines blurred by fog.

My old friend died last night,
my SVEA camp stove,
whom I have lit for forty years.
She perished in explosive flames.

SVEA and I have had good times –
snow camping in the High Sierras
with my girlfriend – our hot bodies
warming us, our kisses desperate
in the valley of death.
SVEA and I have had bad times –
snow camping in the High Sierras
with my girlfriend near Donner Pass,
where snow-bound starving humans in 1846
cannibalized each other in desperation.
We almost died of hypothermia and exhaustion
when SVEA was new and I was twenty-something.

She was brass-plated like gold.
I was always glad to see her
before a camping trip or just winking at me
for no reason, from her basement shelf.

Maybe there are but a few years left for me
to leave a footprint in the wilderness.
I shall miss it as much as breathing.
I'll keep dearly departed SVEA on that shelf,
like an urn holding cremated ashes,
and we'll wink at each other,
my companion in the wilderness,
or the basement darkness.

Long Trail – Sucker Brook Shelter – 12 August 2007

Boots

You must let go of old boots
when the sole separates from the leather.
Mourn the many miles,
the weariness, and exaltation.

These new boots are not yet mine.
They have barely six miles on them.
So far, so good – no hot spots.
I'm still learning how they grip or slip on wet rocks.

My old boots sit outside with the trash.
I think I'll bury them and mark the grave.
Or plant forget-me-nots in them
for one last season.
Old friends who have carried me
to the lap of God and back.

Battell Shelter – Long Trail – 28 June 2011

The High Life

A hot wind stirs the sultry air,
a ladle stirring soup.
Orange moth settles
on broad green leaf,
thinking, without choice
of the next orange moth generation.
Mayfly, who lives but a day,
seems unconcerned.
Mayfly is as old
as this mountain.

Rain starts on the sheer face
of Mount Mansfield's forehead.
A soaking, persistent rain.
And still Moth
and Mayfly flutter.

My son and I look over our shoulders
at the dark cloud clawing towards us.
Moth and Mayfly flutter,
as old as the mountain.

Contrast the learned ignorance
of the scholar, whose wisdom
carries an expiration date;
each savant so recently born –
so nearly extinct.

Moth and Mayfly flutter.

Long Trail – Butler Lodge – Mount Mansfield – 26 June 1993

Erratic

Overhanging Rock,
an erratic left behind by the glacier,
hangs precariously over the Long Trail
between Bear Hollow and Whiteface shelters.
Trees root on its roof.
It was most apt to collapse
the day it was deposited here
10,000 years ago, give or take.
Overhanging Rock may give way today,
but I'll eat lunch under its mossy shelter.

Long Trail – Sterling Pond Shelter – 13 July 2008

Backpack

I carry the weight of my life on my back.
Hard to know which is more onerous,
uphill, slow and plodding, sweating,
or downhill, too fast, too easy to fall.
From time to time I am rewarded
with a level path, brown and serpentine,
through a fern meadow.
For me, respite from the rigors of the trail.
For through hikers, the autobahn
for making up miles.

I amble, no mythic dream of Katahdin,
content to witness the spectrum of spirit, of animation,
from hyperkinetic, night-hiking NOBOs
to a self-effacing granite erratic
awaiting the next glacier.

During these five days,
in this dimension of wilderness,
I am an expatriate, a hobo,
carrying a tent for my house.
My kitchen and stove weigh two lbs,
my bedroom one and a half.

For this brief interlude
I am one of the ten thousand things,
no more, no less,
a complicated collection of stardust,
an erratic walking home.

Long Trail/Appalachian Trail – Clarendon Shelter
30 August 2014

Mount Katahdin: the end of the Appalachian Trail
NOBO: North Bound through hiker on the Appalachian Trail

Shooting star

Late August.
I try to imagine the summer forest snow-shrouded.
My son empties muddy water from his boots.
I wring rain from my bandana.
Shooting Star Shelter, perched
on a broad mantle of granite,
open to the galaxy,
to flaming bits of cosmic dust.
It rained so hard last night
I thought meteor fragments
pelted the tin roof.

The shelter journal, a student's composition book,
invites me from its small writing table bolted to the wall.
This anthology, full as a squirrel's nest,
full as the Milky Way,
each entry a meteorite,
effervescent and irreverent,
a message to fellow travellers,
a flaming footnote in eternity.

Long Trail –Shooting Star Shelter – Jay Peak – August 1993

Trail Names

Near as I can tell
no one reads these poems.
Which is just as well.
I am free to hand scribe each one
like a scruffy, sweaty monk
in service to sanctity.
I imagine my poems stacked
like cord wood in the Long Trail warehouse
with every shelter journal,
every trail name.

"Rusted Root" has through-hiked
the Long, Appalachian and Pacific Crest Trails,
mostly alone.
He points to his pack – "'Tina Turner'.
Sometimes I get lonely."

"Mops" and "Pops" have run 76 marathons;
they're pushing sixty.
Mops binds her feet with duct tape.
Pops' stories are all about running.

Lydia and Nathan went to grade school together.
Still in high school,
Lydia is waiting for her trail name.
Nathan is "Scooter".
But the dreadlocked boy smiles sweetly and says,
"I'm not 'Scooter' anymore."

How curious to carry so many names.
"Dad", "Doc", "Honey",
"Mountain Poet", "Pilgrim".
We dare to choose our trail names,
dare to hike our Long Trail,
leaving our old names behind.

Long Trail – David Logan Shelter – 5 August 2001

The River That Finds You

At the source,
dying to be born in turbulence,
breaking water, narrow channel.
Rocks, rapids,
sudden zig and zag,
water spills over gunwale,
even capsize.
Sometimes we swim for our lives,
clutching for purpose, to disguise
the humble fraud we shroud.
Precious cargo lost in turbulence –
rebalanced by the weight of grief.

Past the gorge at noon,
life's slope flattens,
the deluge widens,
calming though still formidable,
passionate and swift,
hidden rocks to evade,
tests of authenticity, of agency,
hoping we leave a wake.

Twilight, the river tranquil,
low angled sun fire-lights the mountains.
There is salt in the water,
uneasy mixing of ocean tide
as we near the origin.

Battered, scraped, dented,
our vessel durable,
we know what beckons.
We might choose bliss,
float effortlessly
to the source.

Bread Loaf Wilderness

Facing the long ridge
toward Mount Grant
I climb to silence
along the sinewy trail,
through fields of ferns,
mindful of the profoundness
of ferns.
All around me is something,
and the nothing that wants to be named.
But that isn't possible just yet.

Physicists are confident
that most of the universe
is composed of the unnamed
nothing.
How can I be anything
but confused, and skeptical.

Sunlight turns chartreuse
on fern fronds,
translucent geometric,
carpeting the hardwood forest.

Cooley Glen Shelter – July 2005

Long Trail Bar Mitzvah

The brook's cool damp
smells like dawn in my garden.
Baby green leaves, ever shrinking as I ascend,
dappled in sunlight.
Wind washes the forest.
I feel related to the evergreens –
older, constant, mindful.
When did that happen?
Stepping from rock to rock
over the wet spots,
the way I taught my son in a sing-song,
"rock to rock, rock to rock".

My thirteen year-old boy is about
to become a man in the eyes of our faith
in the flatlands.
What he does not yet viscerally know
is that he is on a Long Trail odyssey
from diaper to shroud.
I will bless his head
like my grandmother blessed mine
with challah-soft hands
when I was his age.

A tree down across Forest City Trail,
under the flank of the mountain
Samuel de Champlain called the sleeping lion
that awakens in the heart of my boy.
When did that happen?

Burgundy and white trillium,
fiddlehead ferns uncurling over
brown leaves and green shoots,
the Priestly Blessing of May
upon the head of summer.

Long Trail – Gorham Lodge – Camel's Hump – Forest City Trail
30 May 1993

The Things We Notice

Pre-ordained or Random?
Or both? Or neither?
A dream?
Time goes this way, and that way,
and backwards, and not at all.
On the trail I can accept all of it,
believe (given the benefit of doubt),
that all is true.

I listen for truth in wilderness.
Since we can never know,
does it matter?
Consciousness is thrust upon us
and in our bewilderment,
our desperation,
we choose.

Questions.
Which rock to step on?
What to have for dinner?
What happens after we die?
And before we are born?

After a few miles
I notice the things that live simply,
the things that entice my attention:
a wildflower, a salamander, a pebble,
the sonority of a hermit thrush.
What are their questions?

Long Trail – Clarendon Shelter – 1 September 2014

True North

My compass, though scuffed and dented
points magnetic North.
When I've been lost,
it was not for want of magnetic North,
only my failure to follow the meridian.

Today's Long Trail, a dirt line
through a field of ferns,
is cartographic like the Mississippi River
bisecting the continent.
My compass needle points me
through that mysterious space
where intuition and 'the old ways' reside uneasily
with Dark Energy and quantum uncertainty.

More problematic is navigating my soul
with neither compass nor map,
only memory.
I remember my father's long gray coat
and New York City Stetson,
one of his disguises – not quite
as convincing as a priest's collar.
The first time I knew my father to be mortal
was the morning I walked into his bedroom
and found him on the floor,
in his underwear – doing sit-ups and leg lifts –
defiance against the reaper's sickle.
I was embarrassed for him
and looked away.

And I to my son?
What run-of-the-mill giant am I to him?
My boy, just twenty-one, is also on the Long Trail
but I don't know where,
or how steep his slope.

I fear I may be an embarrassment for him
the way my father was for me.
He needs his time alone,
but I worry.
I pray his compass is true.

Long trail – Skyline Lodge Shelter – 21 June 2001

Whistle-Stop Café

Last night, up the gorge at Clarendon Shelter,
the train whistle, signal from another world,
owl-like at this distance, sounds
will-of-a-whisper under a full moon.

I descended off the trail this morning,
down the rock-fall gorge,
boulders still wet with last night's storm –
a hazardous descent, rock to rock re-entry
onto Route 103, into our parallel universe
of internal combustion and surnames.

The *Whistle Stop Café*,
an old railroad station on history's main line,
has well-earned, mythic status on the trail.
My first swallow of coffee warms and delights.
The train approaches its Route 103 crossing –
a whistle-stop. It wails and I am jolted.
The waitress tops off my cup.
"If you didn't know to expect that,
it'd scare the bejeezus out of you."
She smiles and walks away,
as I wipe coffee off my lips.

Long Trail – Whistle Stop Café – Route 103 – Clarendon, VT

PHYSICS

Einstein Doubted That God Rolled Dice

Einstein doubted that God rolled dice –
his doubt being not faith, but mathematics.
Einstein knew,
in the roll of the bones
lies elegant order,
delicate design,
statistical certainty.

But I wonder,
though we are not privy to the calculus
as we fall through our geometric web,
if it only seems to us,
from our relative perspective of falling,
that God does not care.

Grand Union (2000)

Broadway and Nagle Avenue
shone black in the spring rain –
a city rain releasing
sweet and sour scents
of asphalt.
I crossed Nagle
from my elementary school
to the bodega.
He crossed the other way.
As we passed, he threw a punch
at my face
from under his yellow poncho.
The faint wind of his right jab
glanced off my lips
like a bee's wings
and I tasted danger –
our meeting aborted
by one eighth of an inch.
We passed, but the photo
in my mind's album
carries the sharp taste of
fear that choreographed
my boy's life in New York City.

The Periodic Table of Elements
names the meeting
of protons and neutrons –
manifestations of
the primordial force –
electrons, the light within.
Our circle of Quakers,
our Meeting
of protons and neutrons,
blends our empty spaces
to share our light.

Cheryl spins a tale,
an allegory of sin
and The Grand Union
express check out
(more than ten items –
a long line of
angry stares).
The gossamer fiber
of her ministry weaves
through each Friend, in turn,
like a golden thread
stringing a necklace
of pearls

Oh, that I could meet
everyone on such terms.
But to this day
I am glad not to have met
that boy under the yellow poncho
crossing Nagel Avenue
throwing a punch.

Einstein's dream
of a Grand Unified Theory
remains elusive.
I am content for now
to sit in Quaker Meeting –
embraced by three of the four
fundamental forces of nature –
the strong force,
the weak force,
electromagnetism.
But I do worry
about the orphan force,
gravity,
and that boy under
a yellow slicker.

Empty Space – Dark Matter

Leaf coloured toad
hops away on tip-toes;
orange salamander
slithers and disappears
under a leaf.
A white quartz rock
lined with black veins,
juts onto the Long Trail,
as old as the Earth.
Moss softens one end.

I feel the rock with my boot,
marvel at the moss
and cheer for the salamander.
They and I – all citizens of the Cosmos.
But we are exceptions
to the rule of dark matter,
dark energy.

It is the same
in the entire universe
as we know it –
as we try to explain it.
Dark matter dwarfs the drama
of clustered galaxies.
Without it
the sneeze of God
would expand forever.
We would wink out
like a dying candle,
and finally end in ice.

But if our calculations are in error,
as they routinely are,
the cosmos will collapse.
God will inhale creation
and we will end in fire.
This dark, full emptiness

onto whose gravitational glue
light sticks like rhinestones
on black velvet,
governs our hearts as well.
In which realm do love
and desire dwell?
Is longing that much more elusive
than Quarks and dark matter?
Theoretical physicists,
modern day Merlins,
probe the dark matter
for a presence so small
it may be passing into
another dimension,
not unlike birth,
so unfathomable to the fetus.

In death are we born into a dimension
as cryptic as dark matter?
Does love fill the emptiness?
The implications are lost
on our metaphysical alchemists
who dare not ask,
what would it be like
to dance in the dark vastness?
Or, why do we,
like a slithering salamander,
scurry to hide our hearts
from the dark matter?

Long Trail – Battell Shelter – 15 August 1993

The God Particle

I am fascinated by the intersection of metaphysics and particle physics. When I heard of the July 4, 2012 discovery of the Higgs boson, a long sought fundamental particle of nature, often referred to as the "God Particle," I was inspired to write this poem. The Higgs boson particle was detected at the Large Hadron Collider, the most powerful particle accelerator in the world. Finding the Higgs boson proved the existence of the invisible "Higgs Field" that confers mass onto everything we know by giving mass to elementary particles such as electrons and protons. "In the beginning was the Higgs Field. . ."

They found the Higgs-boson!
Physicists call it the "God" particle,
detected by Hadron Super-Collider
atomic smash-ups
releasing a galaxy of particles and,
in a Galileo moment,
fleeting evidence of the Higgs-boson.

Near as I understand,
the Higgs-boson tells us we have mass,
we are real.
Now we have to dig deeper into the mysteries –
hew a bit closer to our next incarnation of God.
Perhaps the Higgs-boson will explain the Law of Gravity,
the law we are meant to defy from birth to death.

Robert Frost said it well –
"We dance round in a ring and suppose,
but the Secret sits in the middle and knows."
Tomorrow night the full moon will hang in the sky
and arc the night,
dancing round us.
Fireflies will blink with fierce fluorescence.
The Higgs-boson will have its moment.

Long Trail – Clarendon Shelter – 7 July 2012

Fractals On Camel's Hump

How could two Monarch butterflies
dance atop this mountain impervious to the wind?
Fragility on granite.
Corks on an ocean.

How could this expanse of hardwood,
softwood, peak, and valley
grace this rock, this Earth?
Fragile in a Milky Way,
bobbing in a galactic sea.

How could a question that has no answer
guide us from one impossible reality to another?
Fleeting glimpse of truth's vapour.
We have no choice but to trust.

Nesting spheres of beauty
in a fractal universe.

Long Trail – Camel's Hump – Burrows Trail – 20 August 2012

Umbilical Wormhole

Time traveler through infinity,
through physicist's wormholes,
secret passages under Einstein's pedestal,
across time and space,
a mausoleum in the flesh of your belly,
shrine of infinite connection
to your mother,
      to her mother,
           to her mother . . .

I feel the tingle of time
when we press together,
shrine against shrine,
sweetness alive
drenched with desire and possibility,
to create another time traveler,
another rebel against the tyranny
of right angles and clocks,
dodging particles and waves,
to pass spirit,
against all odds,
through infinity.

Unraveling

Mrs. Schroeder, my first grade teacher,
taught me how to pull apart cotton,
how to divide the cotton ball in two.
The harder I pulled the more resistant to untangling.
"Now do it very slowly and gently,"
she smiled like the Buddha.

What could I possibly know of unraveling?
I could only hold tight
and life could only pull hard,
as it does on the young and the innocent.

From that Zen beginning,
linear years spiral forward, accelerate,
smash my elementary particles into
Quirks, Ambiguons and Ambi-valents.
Sometimes the pull eases,
tangled fibers unravel.

I had to leave my motherland,
yield my castle, harvest success,
pursue sadness and failure,
unravel like helical DNA,
so to replicate,
never quite the same.

Long Trail – Battell Shelter – Mount Abraham – 23 July 2000

Underground River

I worm-hole onto the confluence
of Long Trail and Appalachian Trail,
a parallel universe
of nobos, and hobos,
sobos, and slack-packers,
day-hikers and height-likers,
canines and coyotes,
trail magic and Mad Hatters,
meeting and greeting, coming and going.
Family on a fragile trail,
an underground river,
meandering subversively
through a right-angled,
mess of modernity.

Long Trail/Appalachian Trail – Clarendon Shelter – 13 July 2009

Nobos: North-bounders on the Long Trail or Appalachian Trail
Sobos: South-bounders on the Long Trail or Appalachian Trail

Coral Orbits

On the coral reef, neon fish
swim unaware of their staggering beauty,
unaware that water is air.
We, too, dart about in our community of concretion,
our coral reef that shields us
from the gamble of time and space,
generation upon generation,
sheltering from the ocean's deep fathoms.

Moon's full light stabs the water,
scatters off the coral,
pulls with mysterious gravity
that binds us –
moon, earth, water, lover,
small balls of wonder.
Each orbit about our star,
from ellipse to perfect circle,
whipped about with sling shot gravity.

The momentum of love,
whipsawed through space and time,
is compelled by mystery, affinity, spark.
We surrender to the tide that
washes our coral reef
with timeless tempo and rhythm.

Two Creation Myths

I. Iroquois

In the beginning,
before Earth, before People,
all things were in balance.
The winsome wife of Sky-World Chief
fell ever so slowly through a hole in the sky.
The water creatures scurried to make room for her.
Great Turtle offered his back.
The falling wife, soon to be Mother,
needed earth to stand like a tree.
Neither Duck, nor Loon, nor Beaver,
could dive deep enough to retrieve earth.
It was finally Muskrat, lungs bursting,
who reached the bottom.
Up he came with one tiny speck of earth,
that grew on Turtle's back
until it became the dry land.
Two swans swept up the falling woman
and gently planted her on Turtle's back.
From her hands fell the seeds of the first plants.
Oh! What wondrous seeds,
grabbed from the Sky-World's great tree
as she fell through a hole in the sky.

II. Molecular Evolution

In the beginning
was Earth's primordial soup –
ammonia, methane, carbon dioxide and water,
flash cooked by Lightning into First Protein.
And Lightning begat Second and Third Protein.
Proteins danced in Brownian frenzy
until, one torrid day, two molecules begat another
in their own image, without Lightning.
Over geologic time, with glacial patience,
proteins clustered into coils,
and coils arched and turned upon themselves
to form Double Helix – footprint of God.
Thus was created First Man and First Woman.

III. Your Choice

Which myth do you want to believe?
Both, and neither, are true – I swear it.
At each turn on this mountain trail
creation reaches out and touches me.
Each bird call, each pungent earth odour
suggests again the mystery,
but never mythic details.
So we tell the story as best we can.
My soul is settled, comforted by any story
that tames the fury of lightning
and suggests my place,
arching and turning
to be born.

Long Trail – Spruce Peak Shelter – 25 August 1993

SPIRIT

I Am A God To The Birds

I am a God to the birds
flocking to my feeder in winter.
A forgiving God who,
when winter winds bite
and summer's bounty is frozen,
miraculously provides fishes and loaves,
sunflower seeds and suet,
in exchange for their beauty,
their bickering, their blessing.
They cannot know how I praise them
through the glass, astounded
that they can fly and I cannot,
that for them fear is so ordinary,
so transcendent, that they proclaim
the glory.

When the winter of my soul chills,
when the fruits of summer are exhausted,
I turn to holy books to peck at their words
for seeds of truth, for sustenance, for exaltation.
I revel in the mystery, the prayer that a God
behind the window loves me enough
to feed my soul.

First Prize, 2017 International Proverse Poetry Contest

"A Stubbornly Persistent Illusion"

"The distinction between the past, present and future is only a
stubbornly persistent illusion."—Albert Einstein

The stubbornly persistent illusion of time,
is obvious when I consider the photo collages –
when I gaze at my young father and mother
from where they live on my wall,
patient, constant, faithful.

Dad is twenty, a full head of dark hair,
sitting on a dirt road in Italy
beside his rucksack, puffing a pipe.
He stares past the frame, past the smoke
of his pipe into 1938, unaware of
the looming psychotic break of war.
He is fifteen years younger than my son.
Mom gifts the photographer
her Mona Lisa smile, as if just informed
of her first pregnancy, my brother.

I know their crude taxonomy:
Daddy, Heinz, Harvey, finally Dad.
Mommy, Nanni, Nana, finally Mom,
a mere slice of their lives across an ocean of time.
What matters is that they are here, defying time,
as long as I notice them.

In my orderly, synaptic brain,
Past is mere memory.
Present – moment to moment elusiveness,
everything and nothing,
Future – infinity, everything possible.
How many dimensions do I inhabit?

Merrily, merrily, merrily, merrily,
life is but a dream
from which we cannot awaken.

Ellie's Second Baby:
Reflections on a recent emergency caesarian section.

A teardrop of water
opens up where the frozen river
runs under a bridge.
Rippling water trills
the snowy day.
A pileated woodpecker
drums dead wood.
The spruce forest holds its breath –
the pulse of life barely palpable –
trees creak in gentle wind.
Life waiting.

Severed from the roots
of her placenta,
she lay pulseless,
still as deep snow.
The slash of caesarian knife
opens up the frozen river and
Ellie's second baby spills out
of her ruptured womb
through a rent in time,
holding her breath. Rippling
blood trills her deliverance.

Deep inside Ellie
a world of holding breath,
suspended pulse
has saved her second baby
long enough for
light and tubes and saline –
lightning, cyclones, deluges –
to thaw her baby
into our world
of stainless steel

that cannot abide the
barely palpable pulse
of winter.
    Of waiting.
        Of holding breath.

Bread Loaf Campus, Ripton, VT – Robert Frost Trail
26 January 1994

Blood – House-call on the Canadian border

After three days hard snow,
this border town is ominously picturesque.
My snow boots break a path
to seven-year-old Rodney,
who lives in the Charbonneau trailer,
completely drifted over on Troy Street.
The Alberta Clipper's arctic blast
across the Canadian border
whips my face, whips windows wrapped in plastic,
scatters heat like feathers shook loose
from geese too lame to migrate.

The steel of my stethoscope is a shock
on Rodney's chest. His blue-rimmed eyes widen,
his breath sucks in, and in again.
I search for shine in his too-heavy eyes.
What does Rodney know of radiance?
Through my black stethoscope
polar winds search empty caves for blood.
I must believe that his heart still pumps the energy of creation;
possibility still suffuses the capillary network of his dreams.
But Rodney wears sneakers in the snow
and sleeps beside the gas stove
that bakes warmth all night to save on fuel oil.
He'll grow a few more winters
and lose his one-eyed teddy bear.

School is cancelled,
the street muffled by snow.
Until it melts.

Prayer Flags

Tattered Tibetan prayer flags
hang like wilted flowers,
from the broken string that once stretched
across the lean-to opening.
These quilt-square-sized patches,
once brilliant green, red, blue, white,
are inscribed in Tibetan script
meant to promote peace, compassion, strength, and wisdom.
These are not invocations to gods
but prayers blown by the wind
to every creature, every moving particle,
every empty space.

Our own prayers, too, hang limply,
a balm against the cruelty,
the randomness of fate,
the certainty of death and decay.
We know too much and not enough.
So we build grand cathedrals,
synagogues, mosques and more,
to secure brief respite, conditional hope.
Ultimately, it is for naught.
These massive walls will one day fall,

I re-tie the prayer flags across the opening.
I carefully straighten each one.

Long Trail – Swansong [Secret] Shelter – 1 July 2018

Suspended Animation

Pine seedlings as numerous
and luminescent as the stars,
thrust upward for light because they can,
because they must.
Tiny orange mushrooms sprout from moss
on a rotting pine log where
a delicate pine shoot surges
from the placenta of its mother's decay.
Perhaps this one will grow tall enough
for my great grandchild to lean against one day
and be comforted.

Every being is aware of life
(only we are aware of death).
Every being has its season.
I sit on the unloading platform
of Mount Ellen's ski lift shrouded in mist,
the triple chairs stilled in time.

The moment is always suspended,
thus we craft fairy tale, anecdote, memoir, allegory
and epic of before and after.
My fable is:
"Spirit can neither be created nor destroyed.
It only changes form."
I will be back.

Long Trail – Glenn Ellen Shelter – 29 July 2011

Early Fall – In Memoriam – 9/11

I. The First Tower is Hit

It was early Fall in New York
and the first scent of winter
blew off the East River
from *Spyten Dyvil* – "Spitting Devil."
The new boy at Junior High School 143,
from Texas, or Oklahoma, I don't recall,
stood on a chair and twirled his lariat
for Mrs. Block's 7th grade class.
When he was done, he circled back to his seat,
and my golden-haired Stephanie,
her head back, her ponytail dangling,
smiled for him the smile that had only been for me.
Her fingers reached back over her shoulders.
She touched him as he passed
and my heart collapsed.
For the longest time,
intrusive thoughts robbed my sleep.
My chemistry was polluted.
Ash coated my heart
until I fell in love again.

11 September 2001

Early Fall – In Memoriam – 9/11

II. Collapse

Today, the great city's heart is broken
and I remember Stephanie's betrayal;
it is the first time all over again.
Only embers and ash remain.
One month later, a red-hot ingot
of steel is removed
from the rubble's heart.
Strangers touch each other
with their eyes.
Grown-ups write poems on sidewalks.
Children unlucky enough to bear witness
knock down block towers over and over,
wincing, sighing slight smiles.
They will draw angels saving burning houses.
(For God's sake, it's been four weeks
and the smoke still rises.)
In Saint Patrick's Cathedral, devotional candles cracked
from the heat of so many flames.

11 September 2001

The Sacred Is Ordinary

Our backyard gray squirrel
sits on her haunches
between patches of sugar snow
sniffing her dream
of nuts and fruits,
a mate, her babies,
her fragrant earth.

The sacred is ordinary.
Attachment is holy magnetism,
invisible, undeniable, incomprehensible.
Compassion and forgiveness,
bonding forces as sure
as electromagnetism, the strong force,
the weak force, and gravity.
Though unfathomable,
we perceive the enigma,
hold the question like water in our hands,
give and receive from conception,
the spark of connection.

Blessed with bounty we indulge the miracle,
blurred margins, clouded distinctions.
We are ordinary and extraordinary.
We glimpse everything,
the grand unified essence
of this ordinary, sacred, moment.
This moment – now, here.

A tufted titmouse drops
a sunflower seed from the feeder.
Our gray squirrel scoops it up
and indulges in another miracle.

14 May 2015

Receive What Is Offered

Receive summer's bounty.
Serenity of paddling through twilight,
a kingfisher screeching,
swooping before our bow.
Receive January's silence,
back-country skis slicing fresh snowfall,
confection covered evergreens,
azure blue sky.
Frozen trees creak,
running water hums under river ice.

Receive life however it is offered
on our water world,
if for no other reason
than you cannot hold water,
cannot deny ineffable essence
murmuring to us
under the ice of perception.

Just for a moment, discover.
Put aside invention;
your carpenter's bench will wait,
knowing you must return
to work your will in wood
or stone or anything
you cannot break with your hands.

Catamount Ski Trail – Ripton, Vermont

Locked Rooms

Whatever is not impossible, is possible.
These Green Mountains have always been
a mysterious world apart, yet recognizable
deep in my heart, in every ancestral cell.
Bee pollinating trillium, so unlikely,
a matter of faith. Green-eyed dragon-fly
warming on a sun-drenched boulder
at the beaver dam below Camel's Hump,
watching me a thousand times
through kaleidoscope eyes.

When I was young, I wrote stories
of wild children who could fly,
of immortal cowboys catching flaming arrows,
as unlikely as a Boeing 747
or a magnet catching steel.
One by one, the mysteries come into focus,
theoretically plausible, mathematically precise.
One by one, my childish stories were locked away
in a room in my heart I thought
would never open again.

I am an old man now,
and the mysteries return.
The impossible is possible again,
if only in my imagination.
When the time is right,
doorknobs need only be turned
to open locked rooms.

Long Trail – Camel's Hump – Montclair Glen Lodge
21 June 2004

Mosquito

The trail is a mud-brown river
saturated, dappled green.
A good day for mosquito,
if not for hiker.
The air is cool and dry,
the sky azure.
Mosquito hovers in the rarefied forest,
her moment of quantum uncertainty
a *pas de deux* with me.
Freshets of brooks sluice the trail
with inevitable gravity.

Mosquito sucks blood from my forearm.
She does what she must.
Am I so different?
I have passed half my DNA
and my love for wilderness to my son.
I have loved and breathed all variety of air.
Sucked blood from Mount Abe's flank.

Long Trail – Battell Shelter – Mount Abraham – 25 June 2010

Northwest Wind

Summer's last heat wave has passed.
Two weeks heavy with humidity
perfumed by tropical notes
of hurricane Jose and Maria – Joseph and Mary.
(We have a startling capacity for irony.)
Last night's cold front swept summer away
on a northwest wind.

My heat has cooled as well,
swept away by time's chill.
I surrender summer's guile
to crisp air and melancholic
aromatic augers of autumn,
whose inevitability seeps into my bones.
I know too, that autumn will freeze white,
the end of colour, though I have faith
in the intrinsic, invisible rainbow.

Climbing Mount Abe I am sun-blinded.
So much to hold fast, so much to let go,
like a fisherman catching and releasing
the miraculous rainbow trout,
achingly lovely.

There is no understanding,
only explaining at our grade level,
pre-K to MD, PhD, et al.
My world view sprouts
from the Lascaux Cave Paintings
to the New York Times – online.
I catch a glimpse of the ineffable,
the ephemeral, the everlasting,
trying to reckon which is which.

What remains is faith and doubt –
the miracle of our implausibility.
I take grace in hoping the seasons will repeat
in some other dimension,
and I will find comfort
in the ripening of some other spring.

Long Trail – Battell Shelter – Mount Abraham – 3 October 2017

Longing

Last May morning on Mount Abe.
My yearly pilgrimage,
replanting feet and soul,
ferns in glorious Hallelujah!
I'm looking for trillium flowers
and longing for summer.

Every longing is one-of-a-kind,
ineffable, though we try to explain.
I imagine my Grandma Ida
and wonder, what did she long for,
as a girl in Germany before the catastrophe?
I only knew her as "Granny,"
tiny and stout, dried apple face,
always an apron.
I can only imagine Ida's longing
as measures of loss;
three days without stirring soup,
without rendering the fat of a chicken,
three days without prayer.

My longing is the sweet succulence
of morning air in my tent,
the humming of last night's fly,
both of us awake with the sun.
I, too, buzzing boundaries
of primal infatuation with wilderness,
this Long Trail of joy and suffering,
the glory and the kingdom of essence,
stripped bare of baffling reality.

Without longing, the missing grows
long as winter shadows, ponderous,
as inevitable as cold fronts from Canada
bringing rain.

Longing is every miracle
that proceeds without our permission,
forgives us our trespass,
anoints the ordinary with grace,
with gratitude.

Long Trail – Battell Shelter – 31 May 2018

The Brink

On this mountain I am on the brink,
at the boundary between me and
the forest's next generation,
of adolescent green,
trillium and squirrels,
a gossamer veil
covering the other side.

As much as I know anything,
I know Mount Abe's summit,
its rock cairn crown
scraping the sky, another boundary
from whose vantage point,
the sweep of sky and silhouette,
Adirondacks to the west,
White Mountains east.
I am alone and fragile on a windy peak.

Tomorrow my son will be twenty-two.
I feel myself at another brink,
badgered by Anxiety,
gnarled brother of Anticipation.

Perhaps we are always on the brink,
jumping for our lives,
earnest and unnerved,
blessed and cursed.
In our leaping, our immortal atoms
shuffle like playing cards in a mortal coil,
on the brink of wholeness.

Mount Abraham – Battell Shelter – The Long Trail
25 May 2002

MUSIC

Psalm 23/Hospice Volunteer

*I am a Hospice volunteer and singer in a local Hospice singing
group. Our small group sings at the bedside for those nearing the
end of life and their families. This poem is a tribute to the
volunteers who minister to the dying with their unconditional
presence and love. Their generosity of time and spirit is what I
experience as holiness and grace made plain.*

You move through this realm of not quite
reality, not quite illusion,
a song of praise from the shepherd
saying, "you shall not want,"
to those on the journey,
and to those of us left on the shore,
our flock, grazing green pastures to the edge.

In still waters you wash the feet of those
about to enter the valley of mystery
where there are no shoes.
You remind us of the table still set before us,
our cup overflowing gratitude, the restless soul
seeking mercy, comfort.

In the shadow of the valley of fear,
long named as evil,
your sweet song transforms darkness into twilight.
You sing the blessings,
your presence anoints the paths of righteousness.

Can there be a more graceful gift
than to shine light in the darkest of corners,
to bless what has been, and be born
into what always is.
A lesson for living
in the house of the Lord forever.

And I am grateful.
You restore my soul.

Singing Over

I sing bass in __Wellspring Singers__*, Addison County's Hospice Volunteer singers. We sing for people at the end of their lives. We sing people over.*

He nears the end of this journey,
preparing for the next.
Breathing coarse, intermittent,
body tranquil but for fitful breath.
We stand in a semi-circle and sing a hymn,
cocoon a man we know because he is one of us,
and do not know because he approaches the boundary.

Small voices in four-part harmony
fill the dying room, a choir
suffusing renaissance heights.
I know my part well enough
to be present to the mystery,
to see myself in his place,
to both give and receive this comfort,
synchronously.

Grace made visible,
audible,
palpable.

Spring Chorale

The leaf litter is last year's brilliance,
once billions of chlorophyll factories thrumming
with energy I understand as life's music.
Now in ruins, a carpet of corpses
redistributing their atoms – perfect Communism –
"from each according to ability,
to each according to need."

I dream of a leaf, once an exploding star.
I dream the molecular memory of intergalactic gas.
Nothing can be created or destroyed,
only change form.

I query a green shoot,
"Who are you? Where are you from?"
It replies, "I am,"
a small voice in woodland chorale.

Still early spring on Mount Abraham,
thus only timid sopranos and a few 1st altos,
anticipating the clarion trumpeting of trillium.
Their choir appeals to something ancient and wise,
something I glimpse in peripheral vision.

I will never understand the musical score.
At the very least, it must suffice
for me to listen, or, sing
the eternal words we all know,
of Praise and Sorrow,
Love and Loss.

Long Trail – Battell Shelter – Mount Abraham – 21 May 2017

Author's Notes on the Poems

M.C. Escher
M.C. Escher's prints have always been inspiring. My poetic fancy is tickled by his optical tricks and his mathematically inspired woodcuts and prints. As an artist, he too, was inspired by nature.

Anomaly
In J.K. Rowling's young adult novels (and movies) about the wizard-boy Harry Potter, the evil Lord Voldemort is referred to as "He Who Shall Not Be Named."

Battell Shelter, Battell Trail
Named after Joseph Battell (1839 - 1915), credited with preserving Vermont forest land including the Bread Loaf Wilderness and Camel's Hump State Park where I frequently hike.

Camperized
Irony: SKIPPY peanut butter is full of chemicals and preservatives, whereas Dave's Organic Bread is completely organic.

Aquarian
The reference is to "the Aquarian Age" of the 1960s when peace and love was to become ascendant. A reference to the 1969 Woodstock Festival (which I attended) which was subtitled an "an Aquarian Exposition: 3 Days of Peace & Music." Also a reference to the rock opera, *Hair*, which has the song "Age of Aquarius" which became a big rock and roll hit in the 1970s.

Trail Names (e.g. Beetle, Granite Mountain, Mops, Mountain Poet, Pops, Rusted Root, Scooter, Sprout, [Tina Turner])
Most people who hike wilderness trails adopt a trail name. (Mine is "Mountain Poet".) It is by way of honouring the otherness of wilderness, this other dimension of our personalities, that we relinquish our given names and take a trail name. They are funny, poignant, profound, incomprehensible, or just plain weird. I see them in the shelter book entries where I also write my poems.

Poems from the Wilderness
Advance Responses

"The American state of Vermont—and by extension the wider world—has gained a winner in the poet Jack Mayer. Who would have thought that Walt Whitman would ever return? In his nature-reverent, creation-respecting poems celebrating the great outdoors and asking the profound questions pertaining to human existence, Mayer has not only taken on the spiritual mantle of Whitman, but has given it his own always candid, humble and awed veneer, across more than 55 concise pieces. Refreshing, reflective, rewarding."
—**Vaughan Rapatahana**, poet, literary critic, essayist and novelist, winner of the inaugural Proverse Poetry Prize

"Jack Mayer's free verse, like his universe, is ruled by the poet's inveterate unity with nature; he is one with the mountain birds, contemplating an American landscape that shapes his poetry and is shaped by it. Finding sacredness in the most common sights and sounds of nature, he tries to make sense out of memory and time through hiking and looks at man's paradoxical insignificance and centrality in God's creation. From dizzying heights, he surveys human civilization, and its discontents, with a scientific eye which knows that there is something in the human experience that escapes science – something that makes him animate his hiking tools, giving them life, lamenting their decay, and mourning their death. The hiking trails, the memories, and poetry are all things that Mayer has learned to master, yet they keep fascinating him endlessly."
—**Ahmed Elbeshlawy**, author of *Savage Charm* (Proverse, 2019)

"These poems, entered into the notebooks of Long Trail shelters by Jack Mayer's avatar the Mountain Poet, recall such earlier wilderness poets as Han Shan and Gary Snyder. Like those ancestors' dispatches from the heights, they combine reflections on time and reality with the glow of physical exertion in the open air. Mayer's humor also bubbles up in ways that make his voice a distinctive and delightful addition to this lineage."
—**John Elder**, author of *Reading the Mountains of Home*

"Ever since Emerson sent American poets into the woods to discover their souls, the connections between language and spirit have been steadily forged on this continent. Jack Mayer is a writer I've long admired, and in these bright, sensuous, deeply reflective poems we encounter a wilderness that exists on many levels: the Vermont trails that he loves, walks and dreams, and the contours of his own expansive spirit. I read these poems with increasing pleasure, and plan to return to them again and again. Mayer is a fine, fresh voice in American poetry."

—**Jay Parini,** author of *New and Collected Poems, 1975-2015*

SOME POETRY AND POETRY COLLECTIONS
Published by Proverse Hong Kong

Alphabet, by Andrew S. Guthrie. 2015.

Astra and Sebastian, by L.W. Illsley. 2011.

Bliss of Bewilderment, by Birgit Bunzel Linder. 2017.

The Burning Lake, by Jonathan Locke Hart. 2016.

Celestial Promise, by Hayley Ann Solomon. 2017.

Chasing light, by Patricia Glinton Meicholas. 2013.

China suite and other poems,
by Gillian Bickley. 2009.

Epochal Reckonings,
by J.P. Linstroth. 2020. (Scheduled)

For the record and other poems of Hong Kong,
by Gillian Bickley. 2003.

Frida Kahlo's cry and other poems,
by Laura Solomon. 2015.

Heart to Heart: Poems, by Patty Ho. 2010.

Home, away, elsewhere,
by Vaughan Rapatahana. 2011.

Immortelle and bhandaaraa poems,
by Lelawattee Manoo-Rahming. 2011.

In vitro, by Laura Solomon. 2nd ed. 2014.

Irreverent poems for pretentious people,
by Henrik Hoeg. 2016.

The layers between (essays and poems),
by Celia Claase. 2015.

Of leaves & ashes, by Patty Ho. 2016.

Life Lines, by Shahilla Shariff. 2011.

Mingled voices: the international Proverse Poetry Prize anthology 2016, edited by Gillian and Verner Bickley. 2017.

Mingled voices 2: the international Proverse Poetry Prize anthology 2017, edited by Gillian and Verner Bickley. 2018.

Mingled voices 3: the international Proverse Poetry Prize anthology 2018, edited by Gillian and Verner Bickley. 2019.

Mingled voices 4: the international Proverse Poetry Prize anthology 2019, edited by Gillian and Verner Bickley. 2020.

Moving house and other poems from Hong Kong,
by Gillian Bickley. 2005.

Over the Years: Selected Collected Poems, 1972-2015,
by Gillian Bickley. 2017.

Painting the borrowed house: poems,
by Kate Rogers. 2008.

Perceptions, by Gillian Bickley. 2012.

Rain on the pacific coast,
by Elbert Siu Ping Lee. 2013.

refrain, by Jason S. Polley. 2010.

Savage Charm, by Ahmed Elbeshlawy. 2019

Shadow play, by James Norcliffe. 2012.

Shadows in deferment, by Birgit Bunzel Linder. 2013.

Shifting sands, by Deepa Vanjani. 2016.

Sightings: a collection of poetry, with an essay, 'communicating poems', by Gillian Bickley. 2007.

Smoked pearl: poems of Hong Kong and beyond, by Akin Jeje (Akinsola Olufemi Jeje). 2010.

Of symbols misused, by Mary-Jane Newton. 2011.

The Hummingbird Sometimes Flies Backwards, by D.J. Hamilton. 2019.

The Year of the Apparitions, by José Manuel Sevilla. 2020 (*Scheduled*)

Unlocking, by Mary-Jane Newton. March 2014.

Violet, by Carolina Ilica. March 2019.

Wonder, lust & itchy feet, by Sally Dellow. 2011.

FIND OUT MORE ABOUT OUR AUTHORS, BOOKS, EVENTS AND LITERARY PRIZES

Visit our website: http://www.proversepublishing.com
Visit our distributor's website: www.cup.cuhk.edu.hk
Follow us on Twitter
Follow news and conversation: twitter.com/Proversebooks
OR
Copy and paste the following to your browser window and follow the instructions: https://twitter.com/#!/ProverseBooks
"Like" us on www.facebook.com/ProversePress

Request our free E-Newsletter
Send your request to info@proversepublishing.com.

Availability
Available in Hong Kong and world-wide from our Hong Kong based distributor, The Chinese University of Hong Kong Press, The Chinese University of Hong Kong,
Shatin, NT, Hong Kong SAR, China.
Email: cup@cuhk.edu.hk
Website: www.cup.cuhk.edu.hk.
All titles are available from Proverse Hong Kong,
http://www.proversepublishing.com

Stock-holding retailers
Hong Kong (CUHKP, Bookazine)
Canada (Elizabeth Campbell Books),
Andorra (Llibreria La Puça, La Llibreria).

Orders may be made from bookshops in the UK and elsewhere.

Ebooks
Most of our titles are available also as Ebooks.

CPSIA information can be obtained
at www.ICGtesting.com
Printed in the USA
LVHW080721221021
701184LV00022B/1670